CREATIVE NEEDLEWORK

BY

SOLWEIG HEDIN

AND

JO SPRINGER

PHOTOGRAPHS BY FRANK STORK

Fawcett Publications, Inc.
67 West 44th Street
New York, New York 10036

LARRY EISINGER: *Editor-In-Chief*

GEORGE TILTON: *Executive Editor*

SILVIO LEMBO: *Creative Director* • HAROLD E. PRICE: *Associate Director*

ELLENE SAUNDERS: *Editor*

PAMELA RIDDLE: *Editorial Asst.* • HERBERT JONAS: *Art Editor*

ELAINE SAPOFF: *Production Editor* • ALAINE TROW: *Production Assistant*

Editorial Staff: JOE PIAZZA, RAY GILL
DAN BLUE, FRANK BOWERS, AMY MORRIS

Art Staff: MIKE GAYNOR, ALEX SANTIAGO,
JOHN SELVAGGIO, JOHN CERVASIO, JACK LA CERRA,
ALLEN WILSON, JOSEPH MAYA

Stitch Details by Barbara O'Brien

Contents

Introduction

From the beginning of time, men have sought to beautify their environments. Prehistoric men embellished the skins they wore, decorated the walls of their dwelling-places and even put their talent to work in crafting their tools and weapons. This need to ornament our possessions has remained one of the most basic human characteristics. But the once highly personalized job has been taken over by experts—the fashion designers, the interior decorators—even the automobile manufacturers!

And what of the urge to add one's personal stamp to the elements of our physical world? It remains within us, but we have fewer and fewer outlets for expressing this basic need. We no longer build our own homes, make all our own clothing, develop all our tools. We are getting more and more leisure (or so we are told) which we fill with a variety of spectator activities—yet all the while, the urge to participate, to create, gnaws away at our peace of mind. Those lucky enough to have natural creative ability can pursue the fine arts—either as amateurs or as professionals. But for the great majority of us, there is the world of hand crafts to be explored, developed and enjoyed.

Needlework is an ideal outlet for one's creative spirit. A six-year old finds it fascinating—and so have some of the greatest modern artists, such as Pablo Picasso and Joan Miro.

Needlework is one of the least expensive of leisure time activities. Although a room-sized hooked rug may be quite costly, a charming piece of cross stitch can cost as little as 25¢. An additional bonus is the pleasure to be had from producing pieces of possible heirloom quality. In this computerized and "instant" world of ours, an hour with a needle and thread can be as valuable and therapeutic as an hour on the psychiatrist's couch. Few activities are as tranquilizing as knitting to music or the repetitive motions of hooking a rug.

Some people mistakenly object to needlework as a hobby since it seems to be a solitary one. On the contrary, the exact opposite is true—as it is for all dedicated enthusiasts. When one needleworker meets a fellow devotee at a yarn store, a county fair or in a museum, they soon begin comparing notes, swapping patterns and sharing techniques. Needleworkers frequently hold classes for friends and neighbors, and become ardent collectors of antique samples of their hobby.

No longer is needlework relegated to Victorian ladies who swoon at the drop of a crochet hook. Many men are beginning to discover that half an hour spent working needlepoint is as great a way to unwind after a hard day's work as two martinis on the rocks!

Suddenly in this, the last half of the 20th century, we have rediscovered the joys of producing fine handwork. This book is dedicated to introducing you, the reader, to the pleasures and rewards of needlework.

DESIGNER   AUTHOR

The good things of our childhood are captured in this cross-stitch sampler design. (Directions, pages 18, 19.)

Let's Get Started

There really is no reason in the world why you can't start with any form of needlework that is the most appealing to you. You may well be a proficient knitter and now want to learn how to hook a rug, for example. We will assume, however, that you are a novice in every phase of needlework and want to start with the simplest techniques.

One of the easiest ways—and one that is often frowned upon by needlework purists—is to begin with a kit. Of course, we hope that every reader of this book will soon be designing her own projects, but the timid tyro may find it reassuring to begin with a stamped cross-stitch potholder or to fill in the background of a ready-made piece of needlepoint. Stitchery snobs notwithstanding, some very well designed needlework kits are available today.

There are a number of basic rules for needleworkers but there is one we cannot emphasize enough: Do not begin by reading lengthy pamphlets or directions! Let the pretty pictures in this book inspire you but don't read the directions immediately. Nothing is more confusing than the mumbo jumbo of knitting directions, for instance. Directions have meaning only if you have the actual work in your hand. Follow them step by step without reading too far ahead. This may sound arbitrary but it will carry you over some rough spots painlessly.

A PLACE TO WORK

It is the recurrent dream of all needleworkers to have the perfect place in which to carry on the craft—a room dedicated to that activity alone. The room would always be bright and sunny, would have ideal worktables, comfortable chairs, infinite storage space and—as long as we're dreaming—would never need cleaning. Actually, most needlework can be done anywhere—on a commuters' train, at the beach, even in bed when you're getting over the flu! That's one of the joys of the craft.

There is one cardinal rule in this area, however. Always have excellent light. Make sure that it comes over your left shoulder (if you are right-handed). Also make sure that there is no glare.

EQUIPMENT AND ITS STORAGE

Since needlework requires only a few simple tools, it is only good sense to use the very best and to take excellent care of them.

Scissors

Specific equipment for each type of needlework will be discussed in later chapters, but **all** needle crafts require a good basic scissors. Keep yours for your work alone and don't let the kids use it to cut paper dolls or pry open paint cans. For all types of embroidery an embroidery scissors is also useful (but optional) equipment. These have short narrow blades which are sharply pointed. The points must close perfectly to snip threads properly, therefore they should be protected with a little sheath which you can make from a scrap of felt or leather.

Thimbles

For all types of needlework in which a true needle is used—embroidery, needlepoint and appliqué, for example—a thimble is useful. A metal one is less bulky than a plastic one. It should fit your middle finger perfectly, so try on several before buying one. You wouldn't hesitate trying on a great many shoes before buying a pair—and you'll have your thimble a lot longer. In fact, there is great ego satisfaction in owning a really elegant thimble. A gold or silver one is not too easy to find today but it is the needleworker's status symbol.

Needles

In earlier times the homemaker cherished her needles and kept them throughout her lifetime. Today fine steel needles are available in great variety. However, only two main categories of needles are used in most embroidery. Crewel (also known as embroidery) needles are used for stitching on most fabric backgrounds. These are rather short needles with a sharp point and a long eye. For work on canvas, burlap, and other open-weave fabrics where you must not split the threads of the background fabric, use a tapestry needle. This has a blunt point and a large eye. When using either type of needle, select the proper size for the work in hand. The eye should be large enough to accommodate the embroidery thread that you are using but the point should not be so big that it permanently separates the weave of the background fabric. The proper needle for each form of needlework will be listed in later chapters.

Strangely enough, we often become devoted to a particular needle. Keep yours in a needle case, a pincushion or a square of flannel. Even though your needlework may be kept in a large bag, a box or a drawer, it is a good idea to have a small soft drawstring bag in which to store your basic tools. In it they will be safe from scratches and nicks and won't be mislaid.

Knitting Needles and Crochet Hooks

Knitting needles and crochet hooks have a way of disappearing, too. Handsome ready-made cases are available for storing them neatly, but the new

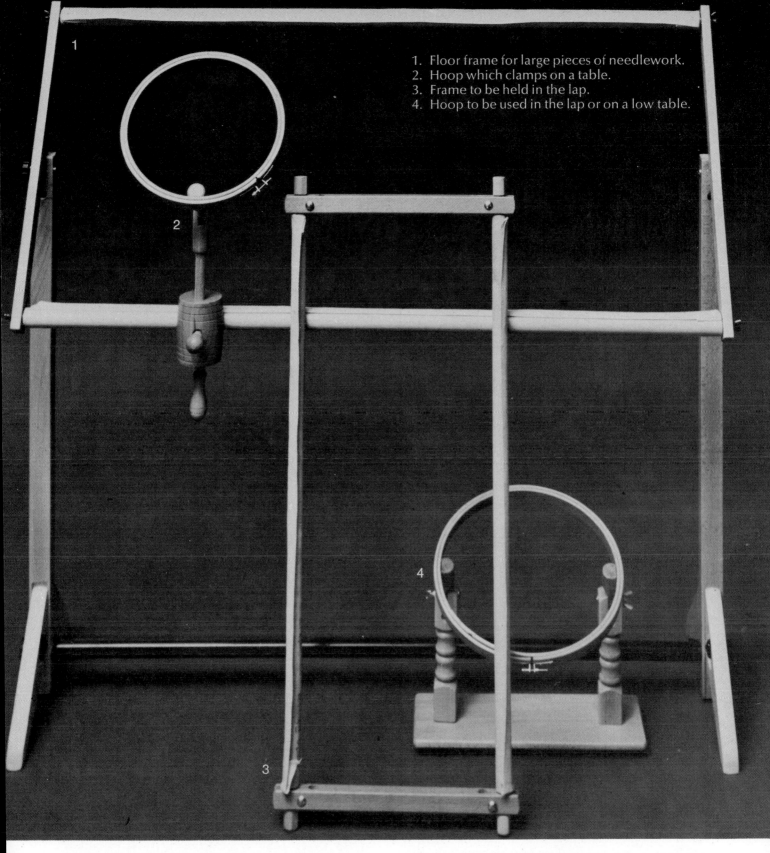

1. Floor frame for large pieces of needlework.
2. Hoop which clamps on a table.
3. Frame to be held in the lap.
4. Hoop to be used in the lap or on a low table.

jumbo-size needles and hooks never seem to fit in them—besides what do you do with that **extra** pair of No. 6 needles? Artists' wood or plastic brush cases make handy containers. Probably the cheapest storage method is one we devised years ago. Just slip your needles in a cardboard tube (an old paper towel roll, for instance) and close the ends with large corks. Do label the tubes—crochet hooks, double-pointed needles, etc.

Frames and Hoops

Most forms of needlework (even some hooked rugs) can be worked in the hand, but your work will be more accurate, even, and unpuckered if worked on a frame. No doubt you have seen or worked with embroidery hoops. These consist of two rings or ovals of wood or metal, one fitting inside the other. The best ones have a thumb screw on the outer ring to adjust the fit to the thickness of the fabric being held. Hoops are recommended only for small pieces of needlework. When used on larger designs, the hoops have to be moved as areas are completed, and the finished embroidery may be flattened. If this is unavoidable, it is wise to slip some tissue paper between the hoop and the embroidery.

To use a hoop lay the work on the smaller ring; place larger ring over it and tighten screw. **Note:** If fabric needs adjusting, be sure to pull only on the straight grain. Pulling on the bias will distort your embroidery. **Helpful Hint:** Always loosen the screw on your hoop before putting your work away. This will prevent permanent hoop marks on your fabric.

Rectangular frames can be purchased from well-stocked art needlework stores. The largest frames can hold work up to 36″ wide. Frames usually have rollers at the top and bottom or have adjustable sides so that they can be used for projects of various sizes. To use a frame, whip the top of your work to the tape at the top of the frame; roll up this end (or adjust side pieces if you have that type of frame) until lower end of your work is in position. Whip lower end to lower tape. **Note:** If your fabric frays easily, always overcast edges first, then fold back edges an inch or more so that you go through a double thickness when you whip fabric to tapes. Finish by lashing the sides of your work to the sides of the frame.

If a rectangular frame is not available, an old picture frame of the appropriate size can be used. Or artists' stretcher strips (from an art supply store) make a good substitute. Hammer the strips together, making sure that the corners are square. With either of these frames face down, center your work on the back, pull taut, and thumbtack or staple work to frame at the center of each side, then at the center of the top and bottom. Be sure the tacks are outside the area to be embroidered. Working from the center of sides out toward corners, continue to fasten work, alternating from side to side. Finally fasten at the top and bottom in the same manner as for the sides. If the frame is very large, work can be lashed in place with heavy thread.

To use these frames you will need to prop them up. Hold one edge in your lap and prop the opposite edge against a table or chair back.

Some hoops and frames come on stands which leave both hands free. If you are using a frame with a stand to be placed on a table, make sure that your table is low enough so that your work is at a comfortable working height. Floor hoops (such as a quilt hoop) and floor frames are particularly convenient to use. They can be adjusted to the proper working height and angle.

Materials and Their Storage

In the following chapters the appropriate materials for the various kinds of needlework will be discussed. But let's talk about storing materials — all kinds of materials — here.

Fabrics can be folded in large suit boxes or other types of packing boxes. If fabrics are kept for long periods of time, it is wise to refold them in another way occasionally so that the creases do not become permanent. However, it is strongly recommended that you roll fabrics whenever possible. This is particularly important with linen. Fabric such as burlap for rugs can be rolled on an old broom handle, linens on a cardboard tube. To keep the fabric roll clean, slip a paper bag over each end and fasten with rubber bands. If you have many rolls of fabric, they can be stored neatly in a closet by standing them in a carton or old waste basket.

Yarns and threads present the most difficult storage problem and there are almost as many storage methods as there are needleworkers. Shoe boxes are fine for strand cottons and small skeins of yarn. Although many wool yarns are mothproofed today, you will want to keep the wools separate from the cottons and synthetics so that you can add some moth preventive crystals or compounds — just in case. Bulky yarns, of course, require larger boxes.

There are quaint cloth embroidery thread organizers available but most needleworkers soon overflow such neat little packages. One way to cope with dozens of small quantities of yarns or threads is to wind them on cardboard tubes (from paper towels, for instance). Keep the ends from tangling by taping them in place. Shades of one color can go on one roll.

Note: Do label all storage boxes. It will save you endless searching later.

DESIGNS AND HOW TO TRANSFER THEM

Once you have become interested in needlework, you will be seeing designs in almost everything you encounter. A postcard in the morning mail might make a great design for a crewel picture. The back of your canasta deck suddenly looks like a handsome hooked rug. Handling the problems of converting an elaborate design from one medium to another is beyond the scope of this book. However, if you work out the various simple methods of developing the designs and patterns in the following chapters, you will soon have the skill to handle more complicated ones.

Often designs are not transferred directly to your working material. Needlepoint, for example, may be worked directly from charts. In most forms of needlework the design is applied to the fabric, however.

To apply a pattern to fabric you must first make

a clear tracing of the design. If the design comes from a book or a fine print, protect it by slipping a sheet of stiff clear plastic over the picture before tracing it on thin paper. Now transfer by the most applicable of the following methods:

Carbon Paper Method

Tape your fabric, right side up, to a smooth surface. Place carbon paper face down on it; tape in place. Position your tracing face up on the carbon paper; tape. With a sharp hard pencil go over all lines of the design. Check to see if you are using sufficient pressure to transfer the lines properly. **Note:** Although typewriter carbon paper may be used, it will be smudgy. Dressmakers' carbon paper is preferable. It comes in light colors for dark fabrics and dark colors for light fabrics.

Reverse Tracing Method

Working on the back of your tracing, go over all lines with a soft pencil. Tape the tracing, right side up, to your fabric and retrace all the lines, this time with a hard pencil. This is a somewhat smudgy method, but useful if carbon paper is not available.

Transfer Pattern Method

Many embroiderers prefer to use commercial transfers rather than develop their own designs. Transfers work very well on smooth fabrics like cotton or linen. Do not attempt to use a transfer pattern on textured weaves, coarse wools, velvets or other fabrics with a nap. First cut out just those parts of the transfer pattern that you plan to use. Make sure there are no loose flakes of transfer ink. Pin or tape your fabric to an ironing board. Place transfer, face down, on fabric and tape in place.

Make a test sample of a scrap of the transfer pattern on a scrap of your fabric, checking for the proper heat of your iron. "Low" or "rayon" is usually the correct setting. Use a firm stamping motion of the iron, not the usual gliding motion. When your test sample makes a clear transfer, repeat the process on the prepared fabric. Raise a corner to see if the transfer is complete. If not, repeat the process. Then run the warm iron over the surface of the pattern and lift it away from the fabric quickly. **Note:** Some transfer patterns have sufficient ink on the designs that they can be reused.

Hot Iron Pencil Method

Few needleworkers know that they can make their own hot iron transfers quite simply. All you need is a copying pencil, also called a hot iron pencil. First draw the design on tracing or tissue paper. Then, on other side of the paper, carefully go over all lines with the special pencil. Be sure the pencil point is sharp so that your lines will be fine. Since the dye in the pencil is difficult to remove once it is transferred to fabric, carefully erase any mistakes with an ink eraser before transferring.

Now apply the design to your fabric just as you would for any hot iron transfer (see preceding method). **Note:** Depending on the fabric, it is usually possible to reuse a transfer pattern made with a hot iron pencil.

DESIGNS AND HOW TO ENLARGE THEM

Early in her career, the needleworker must confront the problem of enlarging a design from a graph. You'll find such graphs under the sections on crewel, appliqué and hooking. The method seems quite formidable but is actually quite easy when worked out one step at a time.

1. Lay out a large sheet of wrapping paper or newsprint, a ruler and a sharp pencil.

2. Check the scale given on the diagram and draw the number of squares indicated, making sure that they are in the proper scale. For example, for the diagram shown, the scale is "each small square= 1″ square." This means that you draw a grid 5 squares wide by 5 squares long and each square is 1″×1″. (Only part of enlarged design is shown, however.)

3. Now copy whatever is in any given square on the small diagram to its corresponding square on the grid which you have drawn.

4. When the design is complete, check the overall design, make any necessary corrections, and you are ready to transfer the design to your fabric.

ACTUAL SIZE

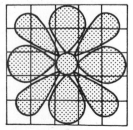

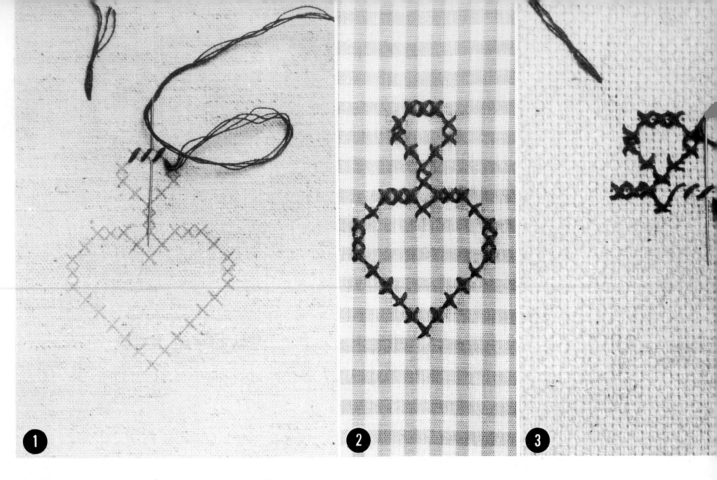

1   **2**   **3**

Cross-Stitch

Cross-stitch, simple or elaborate, seems to go on forever. When we come across a delightfully naive sampler in the clutter of an antique shop, we realize once again that cross-stitch is truly part of our American heritage. We must not forget, however, that our cross-stitch flourishes from roots that range the breadth of the European continent. When we start our adventures in needlework with even the simplest cross-stitch pot holder we are joining a long line of needleworkers who have made the world a little bit more beautiful by stitching small crosses on fabric.

MATERIALS

Almost any fabric from voile to velvet can be used as the background. If you are using the thread-count method of working cross-stitch, even-weave fabric is by far the best background material. This means that the fabric (usually linen) has the same number of threads per inch lengthwise and cross-wise. Other linens may be used but your stitches may vary in size and you will find it more difficult to count the threads of the fabric.

The embroidery thread will depend on the background fabric used and the effect desired. Use a smooth hard-twist wool yarn on wools, possibly a silk or lightweight wool yarn on velvet and 6-strand embroidery floss or pearl cotton on cotton and linen.

CROSS-STITCH METHODS

Transfer Pattern Method

Bring needle up at the lower left corner of a cross. Insert needle into upper right corner. Draw thread tight but not so tight that work is puckered. You have completed a half cross-stitch. Make another half cross-stitch in the next cross to the right and in every cross across that section of work. On last cross bring needle up at lower right corner and insert into upper left corner. You have completed one whole cross-stitch. Continue working to the left until every stitch has been crossed.

You will notice that every stitch is crossed in the **same direction.** For really handsome cross-stitch, it is essential that all stitches cross in the same direction. Some workers prefer to complete each cross-stitch as they go. This is an acceptable method, but we feel that working one half a stitch across a row then completing the stitches on the return trip makes for more rhythmic strokes and evener stitches.

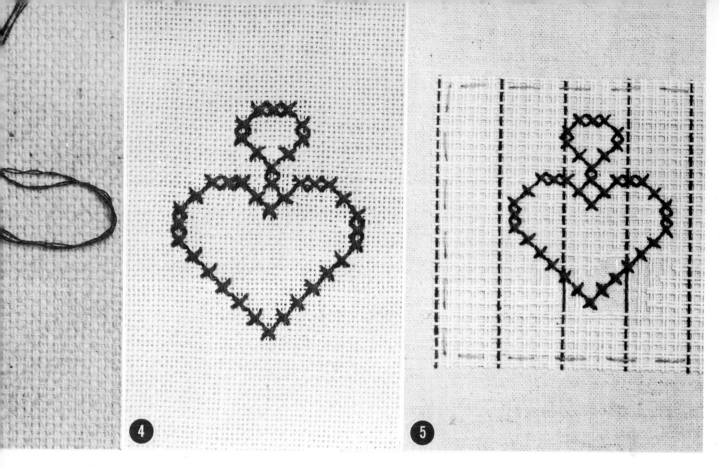

Five ways of working cross-stitch: (1) Transfer Pattern Method on stamped fabric; (2) Checked Fabric Method on checks of gingham; (3) Mesh Fabric Method on blocks of monk's cloth; (4) Thread Count Method on counted threads of fabric; (5) Canvas Method over a temporary canvas to aid in counting

Checked Fabric Method

This is a simple way of working cross-stitch that is highly recommended for the beginner. Choose fabric such as gingham, which has an even-weave check. This method is worked from a chart and no pattern is transferred to the fabric. The checked fabric acts as a guide for the stitches. Lay out the area to be worked by marking with a basting thread. For each symbol on the chart work a cross-stitch in the corresponding check of the fabric. **Note:** Designs limited to a very few colors are more effective than more elaborate ones when worked on checked fabric.

Mesh Fabric Method

Similar to the checked fabric technique, this method takes advantage of the weave of the fabric as the guidelines for the stitches. Some fabrics, such as monk's cloth, are woven so that the threads fall in blocks of equal size. These blocks can be used as a guide for stitches worked directly from a chart.

Thread Count Method

This method will produce the most perfect work and is generally used on samplers, fine table linens and pictures. No pattern is transferred to the fabric. The actual threads are counted, both horizontally and vertically. Each cross-stitch is worked over a square of 2, 3, or more threads.

Canvas Method

When you are using fabric whose threads cannot be counted and one on which transfer or pencil lines will not show (velvet or felt, for instance), this is the only possible method. Baste cross-stitch canvas (also known as Penelope canvas) to your working area. This canvas comes with from 7 to 15 meshes to the inch, so plan your piece accordingly. Work cross-stitches right over the canvas into your background fabric, using the canvas for counting stitches. Work stitches rather tightly. When the embroidery is complete, remove the bastings, then carefully snip the canvas in open spaces between the areas of cross-stitch. Draw out the threads of canvas one by one, using a tweezers if necessary. Wherever possible, snip canvas so that you do not have to pull a long thread through your cross-stitches. **Note:** Even-weave linen of the proper number of threads per inch can be used instead of the canvas.

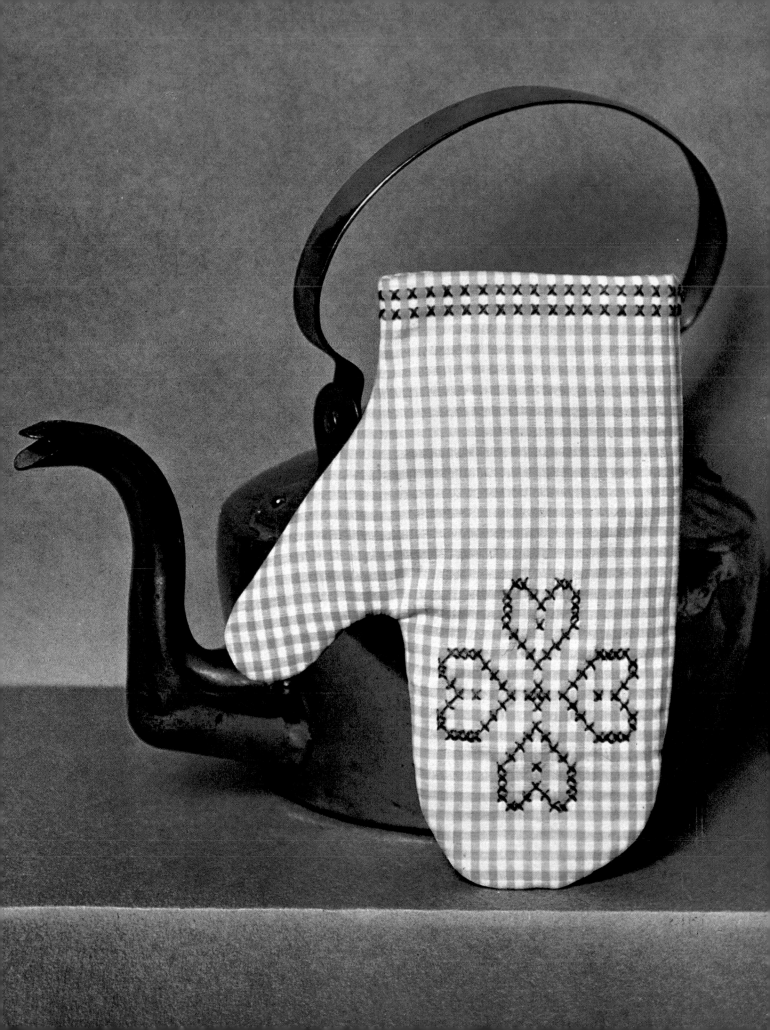

GINGHAM HOT MITT

Many of the projects in this book have been planned to give the beginner valuable experience in learning a particular technique. If you have never done any cross-stitch before, why not start with this practical and appealing little hot mitt?

SIZE: Woman's medium size.

MATERIALS: ⅜ yard blue and white checked gingham with ⅛" checks; pieces of old terry towel or other thick fabric for padding; 6-strand embroidery floss, 1 skein dark blue; sewing thread.

EQUIPMENT: Small embroidery hoop; crewel needle.

PATTERN AND DESIGN: Enlarge diagram for mitt (each small square =1" square). Trace pattern once on gingham, placing wrist edge evenly on a row of checks. Cut out piece in the form of a rectangle, large enough to fit into your embroidery hoop. Place this piece in your hoop. With bright colored sewing thread baste a vertical line up center of mitt. Baste a horizontal line 2¾" from fingertip edge of mitt. Be sure that these lines run right along the center of a row of checks.

EMROIDERY: Every cross on the chart for the design indicates 1 cross-stitch worked over 1 check of the gingham. Work entire design with 4 strands of embroidery floss. Begin by working all stitches on center lines right over basting threads. Then complete design following chart. Now work a border of cross-stitches near the wrist edge as follows: Skip one row of checks at wrist edge. Working on second row of checks from wrist edge, make a cross-stitch in every other check. Skip next row of checks. On following row work a cross-stitch in every other check as before so that stitches line up with those worked before.

FINISHING: Cut out mitt, adding ½" seam allowances on all edges. Cut out 3 more gingham and 4 padding pieces following mitt pattern, adding ½" seam allowances.

Right sides together, place a plain gingham piece on the embroidered piece. Place 2 padding pieces on each of these gingham pieces. Stitch together on all but wrist edges. Trim seam allowances, cutting away padding very close to seams. Also cut away seam allowances of padding at wrist edges. Clip seam allowances on curved edges. Turn to right side; press.

For lining, stitch together remaining 2 gingham pieces on all but wrist edges. Trim seam allowances. Do not turn. Slip lining into embroidered mitt. Turn in wrist edges and slip stitch together.

CHART FOR DESIGN

CENTER

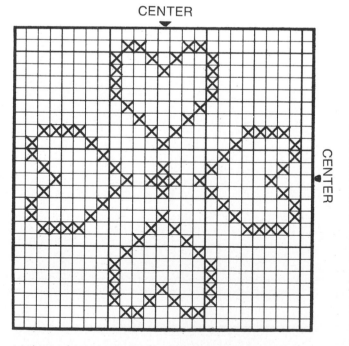

CENTER

Making this quaint little gingham hot mitt is an excellent way to learn the checked fabric method of working cross-stitch designs from a chart.

DIAGRAM FOR MITT

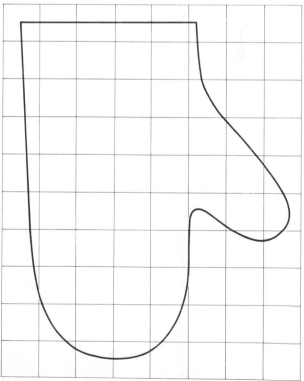

CROSS-STITCH SQUARES

These two delightful little squares were specially designed to help you practice the thread count method of working cross-stitch. Neatly framed, they might add a bright note to your kitchen or breakfast room. Or just the border on Design A would be charming edging a table mat and the center motif could be worked on the napkin. If you are really ambitious, you might cross-stitch the motif on Design B all around a table cloth.

SIZE: 6″ finished squares.

MATERIALS: 36″ wide natural color even-weave linen, 22 threads to the inch (¼ yard will make 5 squares). **Note:** If you cannot find linen of the proper thread count, substitute one that is close. Just remember that fewer threads per inch will make a larger design, more threads per inch will make a smaller one. Plan your piece accordingly. 6-strand embroidery floss, 1 skein each medium blue and gray green for Design A, 1 skein medium blue for Design B; sewing thread.

EQUIPMENT: Embroidery hoop; fine tapestry needle.

PATTERN AND DESIGN: Cut linen 7½″ square. Be sure you cut straight along a thread of the fabric. If you are using an embroidery hoop, cut fabric large enough to fit your hoop. Overcast edges with sewing thread to prevent fraying. With a basting thread of a bright color mark the center lines of square both horizontally and vertically.

EMBROIDERY: Place square in hoop. Each square on the charts indicates a cross-stitch worked over 2 threads of the fabric. Work entire piece with 4 strands of embroidery floss. Begin by working all stitches on center line right over the basting threads. Complete one half of design by working from line A down to line B. For upper half of design turn chart upside down. Omit center horizontal line of stitches and complete rest of chart working from line A up to line B.

FINISHING: Block and frame or make ⅜″ finished hems (see Index).

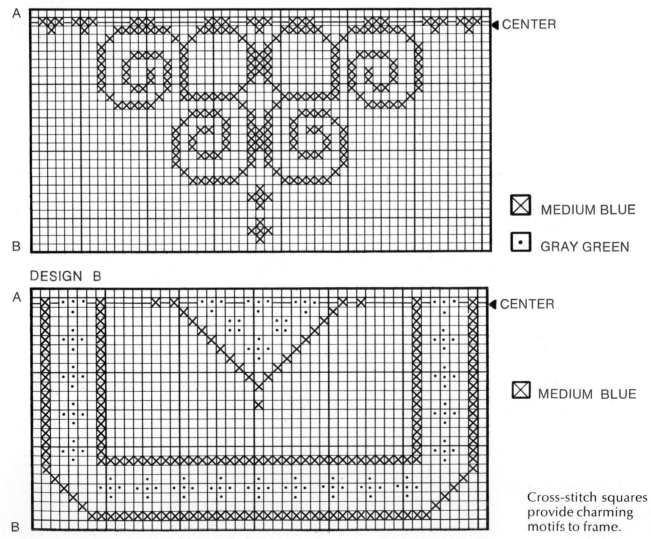

DESIGN A

DESIGN B

⊠ MEDIUM BLUE

⊡ GRAY GREEN

⊠ MEDIUM BLUE

Cross-stitch squares provide charming motifs to frame.

CROSS-STITCH PLACE MATS

Now that you have some experience with cross-stitch you may want to try your hand at a design that requires just a little more concentration. We think the results more than justify your time. These place mats would enhance even the most elaborate luncheon table. If you prefer a luncheon cloth, these same designs can be translated easily into a continuous border.

SIZE: 14″×18″ finished mats.

MATERIALS: 36″-wide natural-color even-weave linen, 22 threads to the inch (1⅛ yards will make 4 mats. See note under materials for cross-stitch squares.) 6-strand embroidery floss, 1 skein each medium brown, dusty rose and hot pink for Mat A, 1 skein each warm brown, taupe and dusty rose for Mat B; sewing thread.

EQUIPMENT: Embroidery frame; fine tapestry needle.

PATTERN AND DESIGN: Cut linen 18″×20¼″, making sure that you cut straight along a thread of the fabric. This large size will give you enough material to attach to your embroidery frame. Overcast edges with sewing thread to prevent fraying. With bright colored thread baste outline of finished mat on fabric, centering it carefully. Make sure that your basting follows a thread of the fabric. Baste horizontal center line of mat.

EMBROIDERY: Mount mat in frame. Each square on the chart indicates a cross-stitch worked over 2 threads of the fabric. Work mats with 4 strands of embroidery floss throughout. Symbols on chart indicate the color placement. Start at the center basting line and work center row of stitches right over basting thread; the left edge of the design should be 1″ from left edge of mat. Work chart from A to B down side of mat. For other half of design turn chart upside down. Omit center horizontal line of stitches and complete rest of chart working from line A up to line B.

FINISHING: Block and make ⅜″ finished hems (see Index).

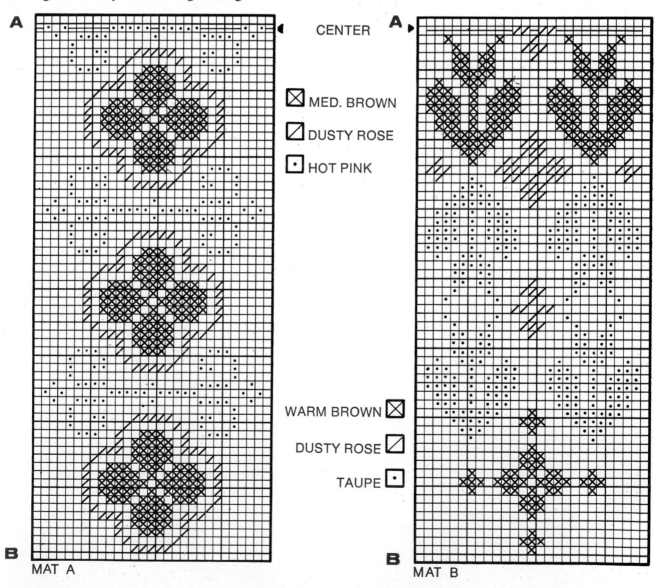

CENTER

⊠ MED. BROWN

◪ DUSTY ROSE

⊡ HOT PINK

WARM BROWN ⊠

DUSTY ROSE ◪

TAUPE ⊡

MAT A

MAT B

Color photo left: Classic place mats to cross-stitch. (Mat A design is shown below, Mat B is above.)

CROSS-STITCH SAMPLER

Although traditionally samplers were made by very young girls, the charm of a cross-stitch sampler makes us all want to embroider one — even if we are just a bit over ten years old. The design of this particular sampler serves a dual purpose. In itself it makes a most appealing wall hanging, with its quaint motifs translated into a fresh modern idiom. These same motifs can be used in a dozen ways. Work just the center flower basket and you will have a picture to treasure. The country ladies or the birds would be delightful on a child's dress. The borders and other little motifs would brighten almost any household linens. Just give your imagination free rein.

SIZE: Embroidered area, about 14½″×19½″; hanging, about 18″×24″.

MATERIALS: 36″-wide natural-color even weave linen, 22 threads to the inch, ¾ yard. (See note under Materials for Cross-Stitch Squares.) Pearl cotton, size 5, 1 ball each red, medium blue, pink; sewing thread; picture frame or 2 thin dowels or brass rods 19″ long.

EQUIPMENT: Embroidery frame; fine tapestry needle.

PATTERN AND DESIGN: Overcast edges of fabric to prevent fraying. With sewing thread of a bright color baste center vertical line on fabric. Be sure that your basting line follows a thread of the fabric.

EMBROIDERY: Mount fabric in frame. Follow chart for design. Each square on the chart indicates a cross-stitch worked over 2 threads of the fabric. Symbols on chart show color placement. Start at vertical center line and work center row of stitches right over basting thread. Although entire chart is given for lower section of sampler, it shows just half of the upper design motifs. Work upper part of sampler following chart from A to B. When left half of sampler is completed work right half from center out, again following chart from A to B and omitting center vertical line of stitches.

FINISHING: Block and frame or make into a wall hanging (see Index).

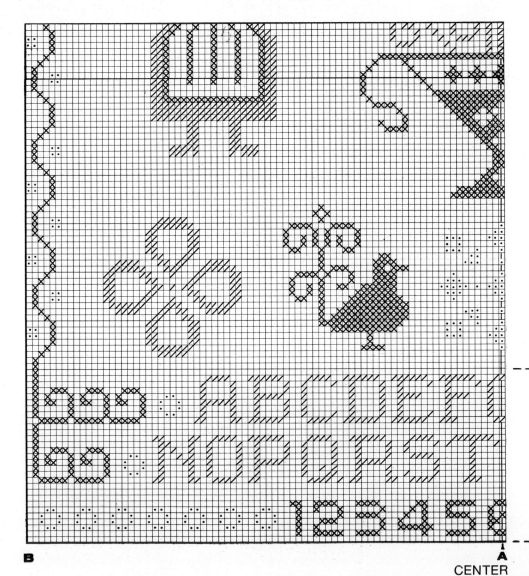

B

A

CENTER

Because chart is so large, it had to be split. When you have completed the top row on page 18, continue up from bottom row of upper chart on this page.

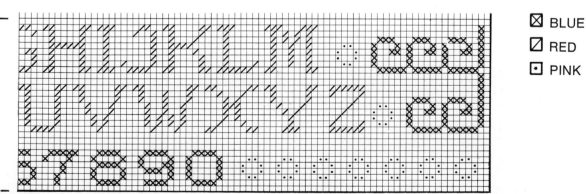

⊠ BLUE

⧄ RED

⊡ PINK

Crewel

Crewel is a very old form of needlework combining European and Oriental elements with a modern American approach—and can be more fun to do than almost any other kind of needlework. Perhaps a warning is in order here. Crewel can be addictive! Don't start a piece unless you are willing to suffer the pangs of a guilty conscience for neglected chores and unfulfilled responsibilities. You will want to spend just five more minutes completing a new part of the design to see how your couching stitch works out. Another few minutes should finish that leaf. And that's the way the crewel—and the time—goes. As the word is used today, crewel is almost any type of embroidery done in a free manner with a variety of stitches and colored yarn or thread.

MATERIALS

Traditionally a twill linen in natural, cream or white was used as background fabric. But there were as many exceptions to the rule then as there are today. Cotton twill, firmly-woven wool, even silk were used. Although natural-color linen is still used most frequently, we no longer limit ourselves to neutral backgrounds.

When we study examples of antique crewel work, we find that the embroidery was worked most often with worsted yarns, frequently with linen yarns and even with silk threads on fine silk backgrounds.

Crewel wool, a fine two-ply yarn with a "crinkle", is available today in most yarn departments and needlework supply stores. Until recently, it was necessary to buy large quantities of each color. Now it is possible to buy crewel wool wound on cards containing only 30 yards. The two plies of some yarns can be split to give you a fine yarn for delicate effects. It may also be combined with a great variety of other yarns and cotton and linen threads for a wide range of effects.

Old crewel was often worked in shades of just one color such as green or blue. Now we work our crewel embroidery in a veritable rainbow of colors.

CREWEL STITCHES

A beautiful piece of crewel work may be embroidered in only one basic stitch or in dozens of different stitches. It is suggested that you practice a few simple stitches to get the feeling of the work. Later on you can enlarge your repertoire. First draw some straight lines (using your thimble as a guide) some curved lines, some dots, and a few circles on scrap fabric of an appropriate weight. Put the fabric in a hoop and with whatever fine yarn or embroidery thread you have handy, practice stitches (see Index). Try a running stitch, Holbein stitch, outline stitch and chain stitch on the straight and curved lines. For really professional looking embroidery it is important to keep the stitches all the same length when working any given stitch. Work French knots on the dots, satin stitch in the circles. Now that you have practiced these stitches you are ready to tackle any of these four simple projects.

SIX BASIC CREWEL STITCHES

(For detailed directions, see Index)

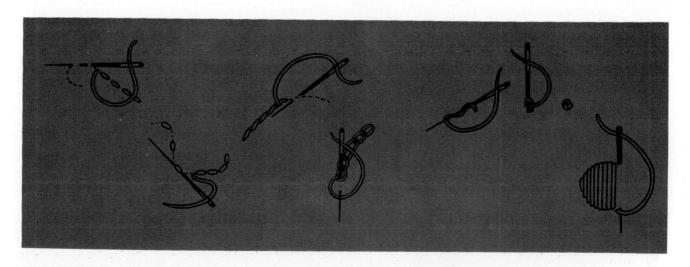

Left: Crewel napkins and napkin rings, eyeglasses case, pincushion, trayholder. See pages 32, 33, 34.

FLORAL PILLOW TOP

Doesn't this floral design remind you of an English country garden bright with asters and delphiniums? Even the straight lines of the background are reminiscent of a proper picket fence. Although the design was planned as a pillow top, framed it would make a charming picture. Or you might make two and convert them into a smashing tote bag.

SIZE: 10″×11¼″.

MATERIALS: ½ yard 36″ unbleached linen or natural-color firmly woven cotton; crewel wool, 1 card each light bronze, medium green, dark olive, pink, orange, dark rose, medium blue, French blue and turquoise; other materials depend upon how the embroidery is used.

EQUIPMENT: Embroidery frame; crewel needle.

DESIGN: Enlarge diagram for design (each small square — 1″ square). Transfer design to fabric.

EMBROIDERY: Place work in embroidery frame. The key accompanying the diagram indicates the stitches to be used. If you have not encountered the trellis stitch, the laid stitch and coral stitch before, practice them on scrap fabric (see Index).

Now start your embroidery using colors as follows: All vertical lines are light bronze. All leaves are medium green with a border of dark olive Holbein stitch. On Flower 1 **working from outer edge in,** use light rose, dark rose, pink, dark rose. On Flower 2 use dark rose, orange, pink, dark rose, pink. On Flower 3 use French blue, medium blue, turquoise, French blue, medium blue. Flower 4 colors are in the same order as Flower 3. Flower 5 is same as Flower 1. On Flower 6 use dark rose, orange, pink, orange, dark rose, pink. On Flower 7 use medium blue, turquoise, French blue, medium blue, turquoise. Flower 8 is same as Flower 6.

FINISHING: Block and make into a pillow or tote bag or frame following directions (see Index).

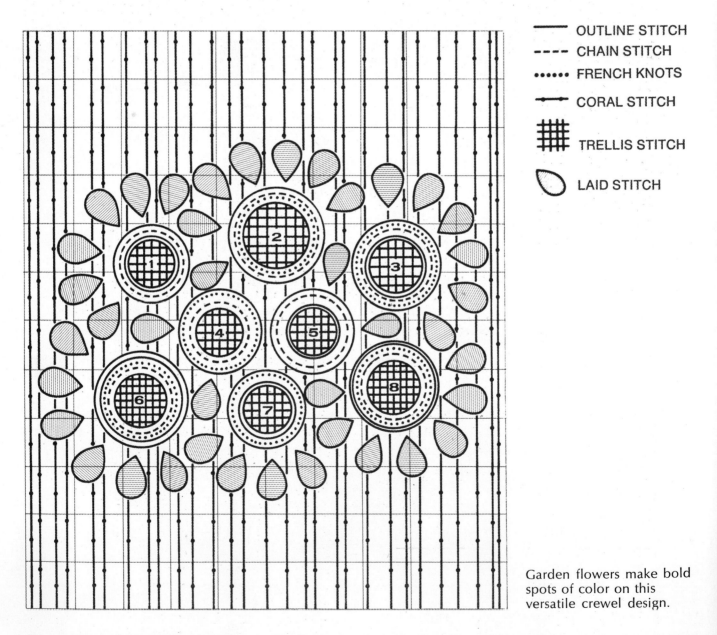

——— OUTLINE STITCH

----- CHAIN STITCH

•••••• FRENCH KNOTS

—•—•— CORAL STITCH

▦ TRELLIS STITCH

◗ LAID STITCH

Garden flowers make bold spots of color on this versatile crewel design.

BIRD PICTURE

What a beautiful way to express affection and friendship! A gift of needlework lovingly embroidered by you would be cherished by anyone lucky enough to receive it. This happy portrait of two doves is symbolic of Peace. The flowers represent Beauty, the bright colors Joy. And your contribution is that of Love.

SIZE: 8½″×17½″.

MATERIALS: ½ yard unbleached linen or natural-color firmly-woven cotton; crewel wool, 1 card each light pink, medium rose, dark rose, dark turquoise, medium turquoise, medium aqua, medium French blue, dark French blue, medium olive green, dark olive green, medium rust, dark orange, dark yellow, brown; materials for framing.

EQUIPMENT: Embroidery frame; crewel needle.

DESIGN: Trace design directly from the color photograph or enlarge diagram (each small square = ½″ square) so that your pattern is the size the piece was actually worked. Transfer design to center of fabric cut 12½″×21½″.

EMBROIDERY: Place work in frame. Use 1 strand of wool throughout. Follow photograph for colors. Broken lines on diagram indicate coral stitch. Unbroken lines are worked in Holbein stitch.

The only exceptions are the birds' tails. The lines across each feather should be worked in a large straight stitch. All shaded areas are laid stitch.

The only new stitch on this piece is the star filling stitch (see Index). Only half of the final little cross-stitch used to hold the larger stitches together was worked on this piece, however. These are worked on all the little star-shaped motifs on the diagram.

FINISHING: Block and frame picture following directions (see Index).

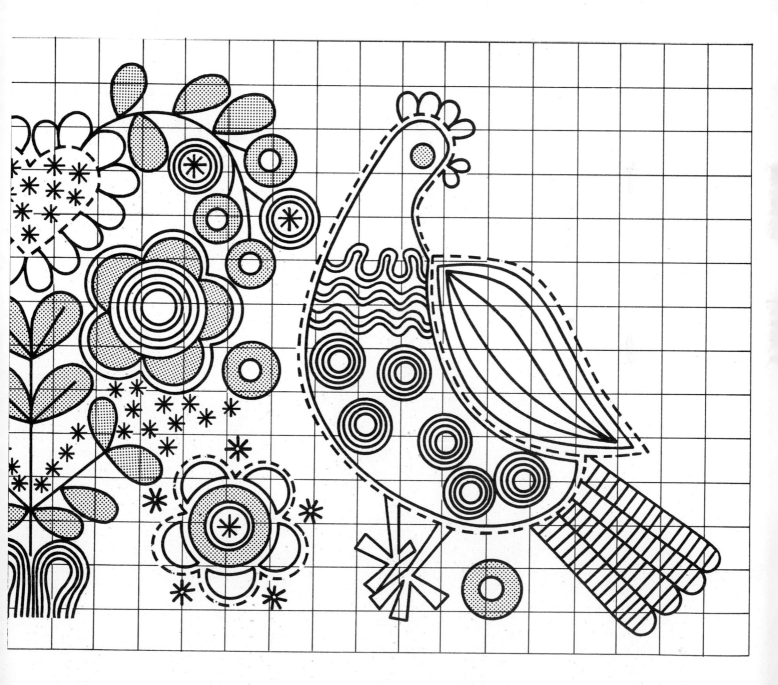

WALL HANGING

Even the most modern room setting would be enhanced by this design of stylized tulips, daisies and asters. Just two basic stitches worked in only one color—rich warm brown—will produce a piece of needlework that is truly in the heirloom category.

SIZE: 19″ x 21″.

MATERIALS: ⅝ yard unbleached linen or natural-color firmly woven cotton; warm brown color linen or cotton-and-rayon thread or crewel wool or pearl cotton, size 5 (see below for amounts).

EQUIPMENT: Embroidery frame; crewel needle.

DESIGN: Enlarge diagram (each small square = ½″ square). Complete other half of design. Transfer to fabric.

EMBROIDERY: Place work in frame. Actual piece was worked with 1 strand of cotton-and-rayon thread. Since you may be using any of a variety of threads, try using 1, 2 and 3 strands. When you have found the effect you prefer, work with that number of strands throughout. **Note:** Since the amount of thread needed to complete the wall hanging depends on the number of strands you are using, be sure to start with a sufficient amount. Unused skeins or balls can often be returned to the store for refund.

Work all lines in stem stitch (see Index). All dots are in French knots.

FINISHING: Block and make into a wall hanging following directions (see Index).

Only one color and two simple embroidery stitches add up to a hanging worthy of a place of honor on any wall.

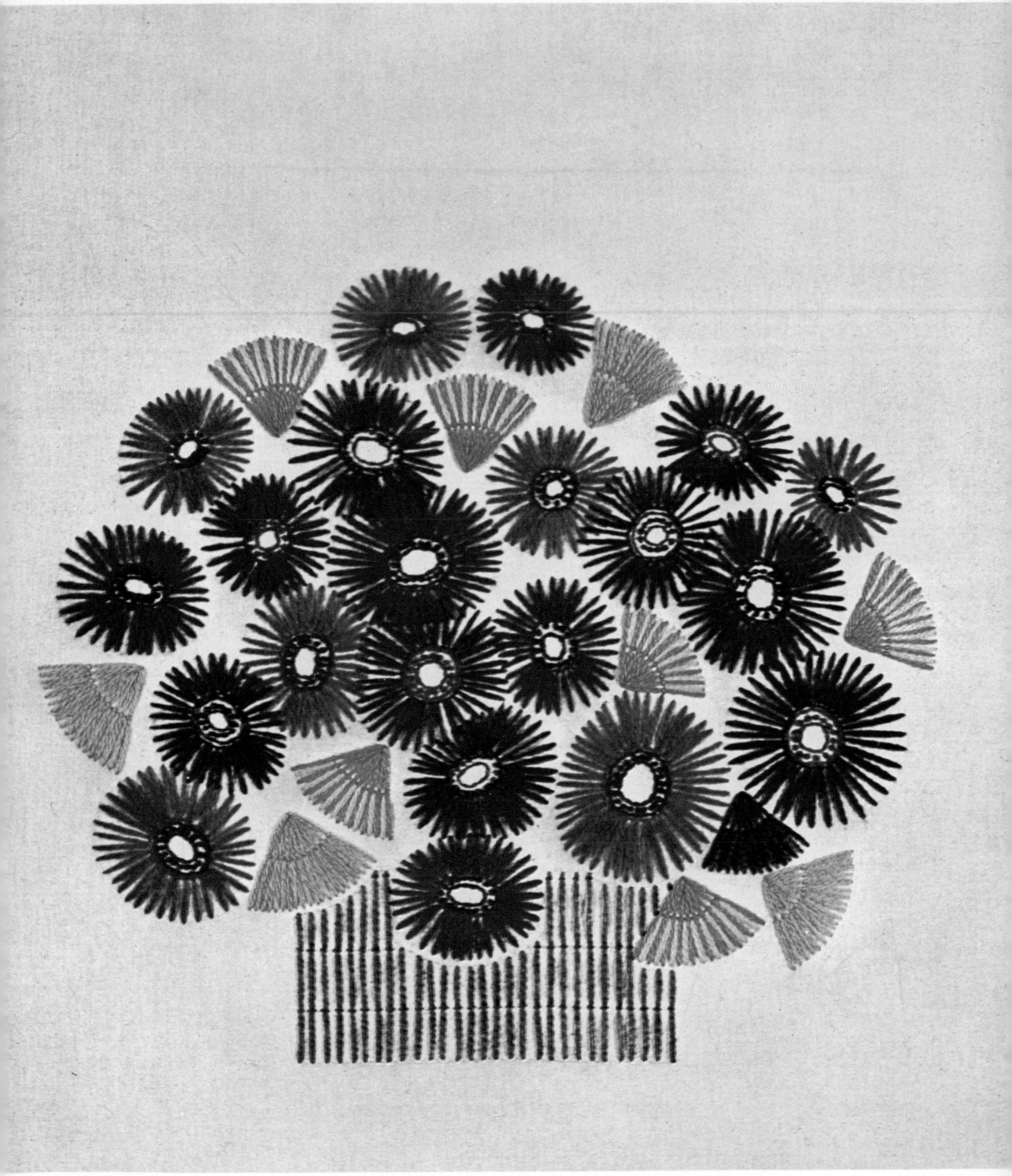

FLOWER BASKET

If Peter Piper had had the good sense to pick some pretty posies instead of those nasty pickled peppers, millions of tongue-tied kids might have had an easier time of it through the years. If you have a chance to try these pretty posies yourself, you'll end up with a delightful wall hanging or picture in short order. The giant stitches work up in no time. Although they are easy enough for the beginner, even the experienced needleworker will find them fun to do.

SIZE: 15″×17″ (embroidered area only).

MATERIALS: ⅝ yard 36″ unbleached linen or natural-color firmly woven cotton; crewel wool, 1 card each dark orange, bright orange, dark yellow, dark red, burgundy, dark rose, bright rose, tea rose, pink, grape, marine blue.

EQUIPMENT: Embroidery frame; crewel needle.

DESIGN: Enlarge diagram for design (each small square = 1″ square). **Note:** Shading on flowers indicates nothing and was used only to make the diagram easier to follow. Plan fabric size needed for the project you are making, adding all necessary seam or turn-under allowances, etc. Transfer design to fabric.

EMBROIDERY: Place work in embroidery frame. Use 2 strands of yarn for all stitches except French knots (for which you use 3 strands). See Index for all stitches. First work petals of all round flowers in straight stitch. To save yarn as well as make stitches neater, work these on the surface only, somewhat like the method used in working laid stitch. Use the color indicated by number in center of flower. Using same color as petals, work a circle of Holbein stitch around inner edge of petals. Now finish flower centers with circles of Holbein stitch and French knots in colors as follows: Flower 1—dark red; flower 2—burgundy; flower 3—bright orange; flower 4—grape.

Work the fan-shaped blossoms (in color indicated by number) in 8 to 10 straight stitches the full length of the blossom. Anchor these down with Holbein stitch worked where the curved line is shown on diagram. Now on outer half of each blossom work a straight stitch between each of those worked before in colors as follows: On blossom 4 use grape; on blossom 5 use pink; on blossom 6 use dark yellow.

Work basket in marine blue in straight stitches the full height indicated on diagram. Anchor with running stitches worked across the basket as indicated by broken lines.

FINISHING: Block piece. Remove from frame and finish as wall hanging or picture (for directions, see Index).

1 BRIGHT ROSE

2 DARK ROSE

3 DARK RED

4 BURGUNDY

5 TEA ROSE

6 DARK ORANGE

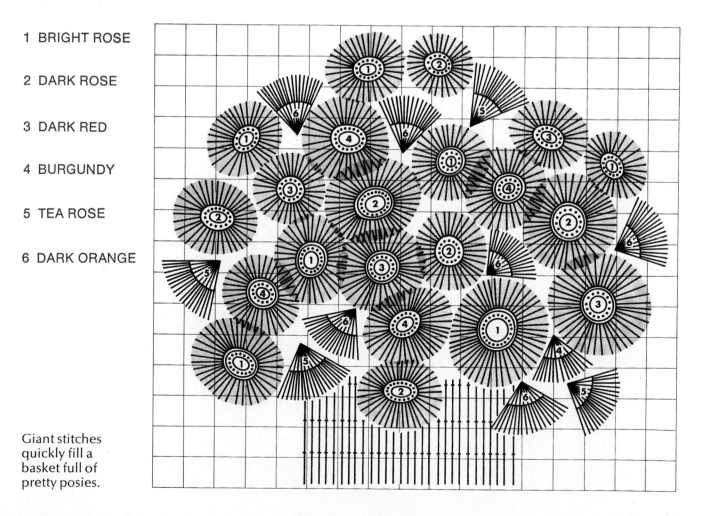

Giant stitches quickly fill a basket full of pretty posies.

31

NAPKINS AND NAPKIN RINGS

Bright colored inexpensive napkins become conversation pieces with the addition of just a few embroidery stitches and their own matching napkin rings. In fact, when you become proficient at making these, you may want to use them as your contribution to the next bazaar.

SIZE: Napkin ring is 1½″ wide, 5¼″ around.
MATERIALS: Ready-made linen napkins (1 extra napkin will make about 10 napkin rings); pearl cotton, size 5, in 2 colors; dressmakers' iron-on interfacing, 1½″×5¼″ for each napkin ring; sewing thread to match napkins. **Color Note:** Napkins shown were worked in brown and white on turquoise, and pink and red on bright yellow-green. Choose your color combination to harmonize with your china, your dining room decor or a favorite tablecloth.

EQUIPMENT: Embroidery hoop; crewel needle.

Napkins

DESIGN: Transfer design (shown full size) to corner of your napkin, placing it 1″ from edges.
EMBROIDERY: Place napkin in embroidery hoop. Work lines in Holbein stitch in light shade, dots in French knots in dark color.

Napkin Rings

PATTERN AND DESIGN: On extra napkin mark areas 3¾″×6¼″ for number of napkin rings desired. In center of each marked area transfer design (shown full size).
EMBROIDERY: Do not cut out napkin rings. Place entire napkin in hoop and embroider all your rings before cutting out any of them. Work straight lines in Holbein stitch in light shade, dots in French knots in dark color. Complete by threading center line of stitches with dark color (see Index for double-threaded Holbein stitch).

FINISHING: Block piece. Cut out napkin rings. Cut interfacing 1½″×5¼″. Centering an interfacing piece on back of each embroidered piece, iron in place. Fold long edges of fabric to back; turn under one long raw edge, overlapping other raw edge and blindstitch in place. Turn in raw ends of fabric. Whip the two ends of napkin ring together.

PINCUSHION

There is something delightfully Victorian about a pincushion. No doubt we use pins as often as our ancestors—and therefore need a pincushion just as much—but they never seem quite twentieth century. Perhaps you'll sit a bit more primly with your feet neatly propped on a footstool when you embroider this plump little barrel pincushion.

SIZE: 2½″ in diameter, 2½″ high.
MATERIALS: Small piece (about 10″ square) unbleached linen or natural-color firmly-woven cotton; crewel wool, 1 card each bright green, forest green, chartreuse; small piece of stiff buckram; scrap cardboard; white glue; sawdust, cut-up nylon stockings or cotton batting for stuffing; sewing thread.
EQUIPMENT: Embroidery hoop; crewel needle.
PATTERN AND DESIGN: On fabric draw an area 2½″×8″, marking it on the straight of the goods. Do not cut out. Following diagram, work out design repeating from A to B four times. Design on diagram is shown full scale. Transfer design to marked area on fabric.

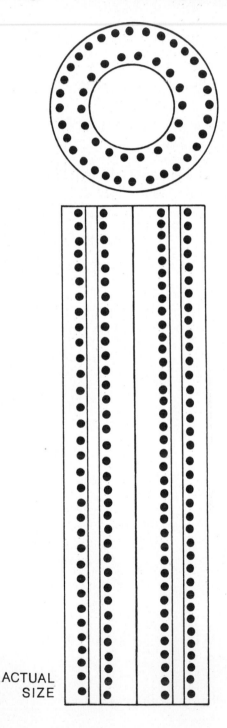

ACTUAL SIZE

EMBROIDERY: Place piece in hoop. The only new stitches you will encounter are the single-threaded Holbein stitch and straight stitch (see Index). Embroider as follows: Work spoke design in 1 strand, all others in 2. Work spoke design in about 16 straight stitches in bright green. Work all broken lines in Holbein stitch. Border lines are forest green; vertical lines, bright green. Thread all the vertical Holbein stitches (not the border) with forest green. On double straight lines use chartreuse and work chain stitch. Work all dots in French knots; join them with forest green running stitch.

FINISHING: When complete, block then cut out strip, adding ½" seam allowances on all edges. Also cut out 2 fabric circles each 3½" in diameter. Cut buckram 2½"×8". Center it on back of embroidered piece. Fold seam allowances over buckram and fasten with a few spots of glue. Join narrow ends of embroidered piece, right side out, and whip together. Cut 2 cardboard circles 2½" in diameter. From center of one circle cut out a 1¾" circle and discard it, leaving only a narrow ring.

Run a double shirred thread near edge of each fabric circle. Place cardboard circle in center of wrong side of a fabric circle. Draw seam allowance over cardboard and pull up shirring thread. Repeat with cardboard ring and other fabric circle.

Whip covered circle to lower edge of embroidered piece. Stuff pincushion firmly. Whip covered ring to top edge of pincushion.

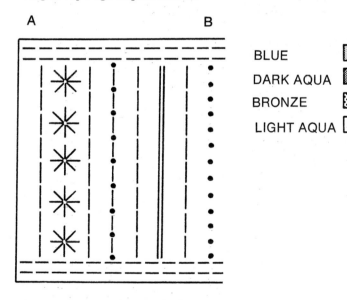

BLUE
DARK AQUA
BRONZE
LIGHT AQUA

EYEGLASSES CASE

A handsome case for eyeglasses is always a welcome gift. This one uses modern colors in a particularly interesting mosaic pattern. Note how placing the stitches vertically and then horizontally makes the design seem to be in a dozen colors, when actually only four are used.

SIZE: 3"×6".

MATERIALS: Small amount unbleached linen or firmly-woven natural-color cotton; crewel wool, 1 card each of light aqua, dark aqua, blue and bronze; small amount stiff buckram; white glue; sewing thread.

EQUIPMENT: Embroidery hoop; crewel needle.

PATTERN AND DESIGN: On fabric draw an area 3"×6", marking it on the straight of goods. Do not cut out. Trace design as on diagram. (Diagram shows one half of design full scale.) Repeat from A to B once again for other half of design. Transfer design to marked area on fabric.

EMBROIDERY: Place work in hoop. Following the key accompanying diagram for colors, using 1 strand of wool, work squares in satin stitch throughout. The direction of the double lines in each square on diagram indicates the direction your satin stitches should take. Work dots in 2 strands of blue in French knots. With 1 strand of dark aqua work a row of Holbein stitch on each side of French knots.

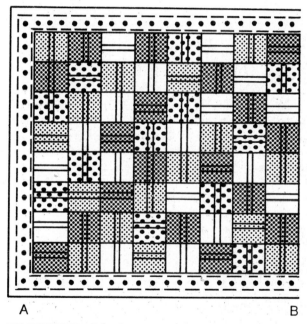

A   B

FINISHING: Block then cut out embroidered piece, adding ½" seam allowance on all edges. Cut 3 more pieces of fabric the same size as the embroidered piece, including seam allowances. Cut out 2 pieces of buckram 3"×6".

Center a buckram piece on the back of the embroidered piece. Fold seam allowances over buckram and fasten with a few spots of glue. Turn in seam allowances of a fabric piece and press. Whip this piece to the back of embroidered piece with wrong sides together.

Center a buckram piece on a plain piece and glue seam allowances as before. Join remaining plain piece to it as you did for the embroidered piece. Now right sides out, pin together carefully the front and the back of the eyeglasses case at the 4 corners. Whip together along one side, across the lower edge and up the other side.

TRAY HOLDER

Here's a project that will not only help you develop your crewel techniques but will also mystify your friends! We'll bet ten skeins of wool that they will never guess what you are making unless you enlighten them. Isn't this a wonderful way to turn a good looking serving tray into a handsome wall decoration? At the same time it is always ready for use. If you prefer, this same design may be adapted to a belt or bands for a luggage rack.

SIZE: To hold a tray up to 15″ wide.

MATERIALS: ⅜ yard 54″ unbleached linen or natural-color firmly-woven cotton; crewel wool, 1 card each olive, light olive, orange, scarlet, magenta, dark blue, blue and turquoise; ¼ yard dressmaker's non-woven interfacing; sewing thread; plastic bracelet.

EQUIPMENT: Embroidery hoop; crewel needle.

PATTERN AND DESIGN: In center of fabric draw 2 strips 3½″×40″, marking them on straight of goods. Do not cut out. Trace design on diagram. (Diagram shows one half of the design full scale.) Then complete the design by repeating from A to B in diagram once again. Down the center of the 2 strips transfer the design, starting 2¼″ from one end.

EMBROIDERY: Place work in embroidery hoop. Use 1 strand of the crewel wool throughout. In the colors shown on diagram work all lines in Holbein stitch. Stems and scroll-like leaves on the tulips are single-threaded Holbein stitch, the threading worked in light olive. All spiky elements worked in turquoise are straight stitch. Dots are French knots.

FINISHING: Block then cut out strips and 2 lining pieces 3¼″×39¾″. Also cut 2 pieces of interfacing 2″×39″, piecing as necessary. Center on back of embroidered pieces. Turn in ½″ seam allowances on both pieces; baste. Also turn in ½″ seam allowances all around both lining pieces. Slip stitch a plain lining to each embroidered piece. Lining is slightly smaller all around, therefore the embroidered pieces must be eased to the lining pieces. This will cause the finished strips to fold without wrinkles.

Wind dark blue yarn around bracelet so that it is completely covered. Tie ends or fasten with white glue or masking tape. Run an embroidered band through bracelet and whip ends together, working on wrong side, to form ring. Repeat with other band.

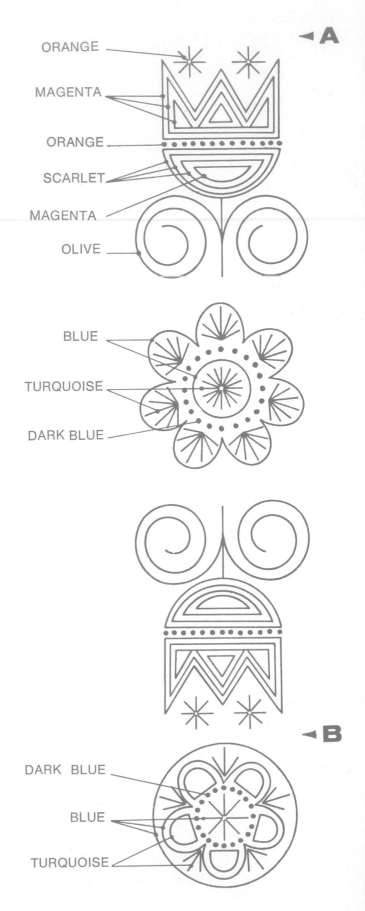

ORANGE
MAGENTA
ORANGE
SCARLET
MAGENTA
OLIVE

◄ A

BLUE
TURQUOISE
DARK BLUE

◄ B

DARK BLUE
BLUE
TURQUOISE

A Sampler of Embroidery Stitches

A Sampler of Embroidery Stitches

Having a wide variety of embroidery stitches at your fingertips is a little like having a large vocabulary. Although we can manage to communicate with a limited vocabulary, we become twice as interesting—maybe twice as smart—when we broaden our choice of words. You can do lovely embroidery even if you know only three or four stitches, but think of the excitement you can add to your needlework when you know the perfect stitch for a particular effect that you want.

In the Crewel section it was suggested that you familiarize yourself with running, Holbein, outline, chain and satin stitches as well as French knots.

Of course, cross-stitch is basic, too. Your repertoire of stitches can now be broadened to include many other fascinating stitches. Don't try to learn them all at once. It would be both boring and confusing. Practice one or two at a time until you become expert.

You may enjoy making a sampler of stitches. Mark 4″ squares on a long strip of fabric. When you have filled each square with a different stitch you will really know your stitches. And the sampler will be a charming memento of the days before you became an expert.

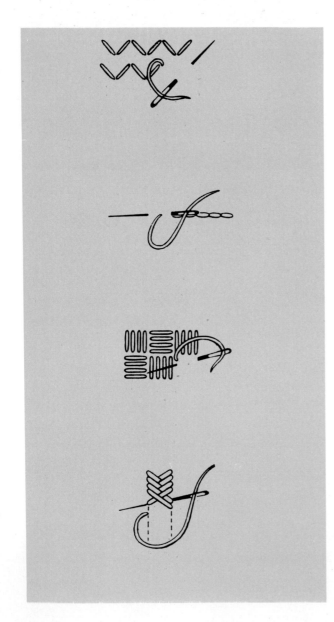

Arrowhead Stitch: This stitch is used for medium-width lines and for light filling. Bring needle up at top left corner, insert it below and to the right, then bring it out to the right on top line. For the second part of stitch insert needle back close to center of stitch and bring it out close to where thread emerges.

Backstitch: This stitch is a basic one used for lines, outlines and as a foundation for other stitches. Work from right to left. Bring needle up a short distance from beginning of the line to be covered; insert it at beginning of line. Bring needle out an equal distance ahead along line; draw it through. Stitches should be very evenly spaced. **Note:** Backstitch can be threaded for a more decorative effect (see Holbein Stitch, Single-Threaded and Holbein Stitch, Double-Threaded).

Basket Filling Stitch: This stitch is used to fill in the centers of large flowers or other areas. Alternate blocks of vertical satin stitches with blocks of horizontal satin stitches. Blocks can be made up of 3, 4 or more threads but all blocks must have the same number. Stitches may be touching or just slightly apart.

Basket Stitch: This stitch is used for solid lines and borders. Work from the top down. Bring needle up on left line; insert it lower down on right line and bring it out directly opposite on left line. Then insert needle on right line above stitch just made; bring out on left just below where thread just emerged. Insert needle on right line below lowest stitch and bring out exactly opposite. Take a stitch as shown, working in same holes that other stitches were worked into. Repeat these last 2 steps. The needle takes a step forward and backward alternately.

Blanket Stitch: This stitch is used for covering a turned-over edge (or a raw edge that will not fray). It is also used for outline or, when worked in a circle, to form flowers. Work from left to right. Bring needle up on lower line. Hold thread down with left thumb. Insert needle a little to the right of starting point but on upper line; bring out directly below on lower line; draw needle through over loop of thread.

Braid Stitch: This stitch is used for borders. Work from right to left. Bring needle up on lower line. Make a loop of thread as shown; hold down with left thumb, insert needle through loop and in fabric on top line; bring out on lower line. Pull loop on needle tight but not so tight that you lose the braid effect.

Braid Stitch, Edging: This stitch is worked along a hem or turned-over edge. Work from right to left. Bring needle to right side just below edge. Loop thread as shown, insert needle through loop, then behind fabric. Bring out a short distance below edge and over working thread. Pull thread through and away from you.

Brick Stitch: This stitch is used to fill in an entire area. Work straight stitches in a row, leaving the width of a stitch between each 2 stitches. Work a second row of the same size stitches but place them so that they interlock with the stitches of the previous row as shown. Completed stitches look like a section of brick wall.

Bullion Stitch: This stitch is used for a heavy encrusted effect especially when worked in gold or silver threads. The stitches are also often overlapped in a circle to form a rosebud. Bring thread up to right side of fabric; insert needle back the distance of the stitch desired, bring up in same spot thread first emerged. Do not draw needle through. Wind thread around point of needle (6 or 7 times or according to length of stitch required). Place left thumb on twists; draw needle and thread through the fabric and the twists. Pull needle and thread to the right and tighten by pulling working thread. Then insert needle through to the back as shown.

Buttonhole Stitch: This stitch is used to cover turned-over or raw edges or to outline. Examples are buttonholes, scallops, cutwork, lines and borders. Work the same as Blanket Stitch but work the stitches closer together.

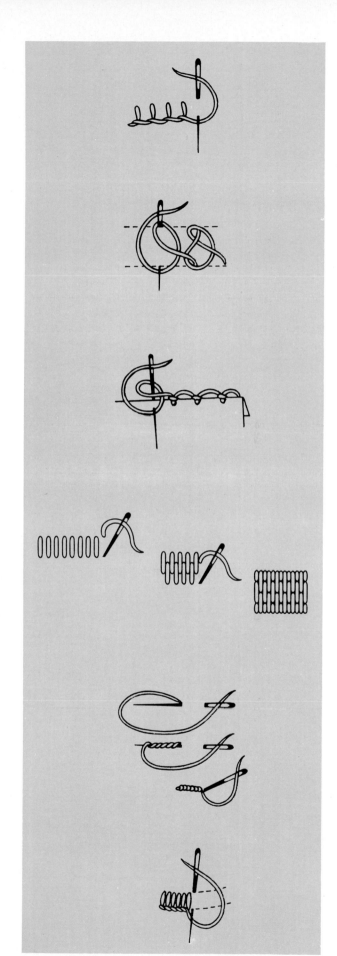

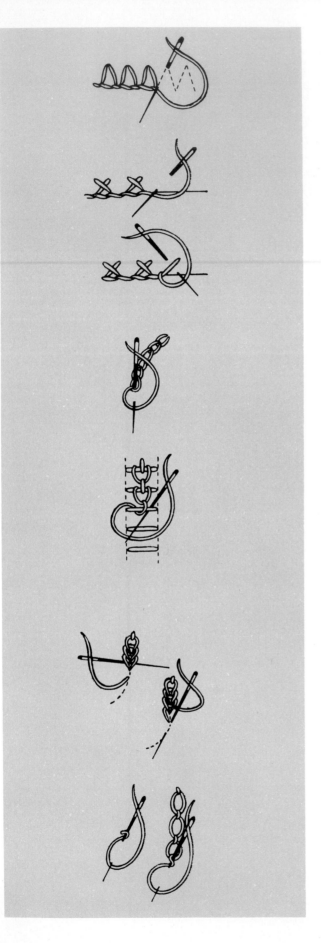

Buttonhole Stitch, Closed: This stitch is used for decorative borders and hems. Work the stitch the same as for blanket stitch but have the needle enter the fabric at the same spot for each pair of stitches.

Buttonhole Stitch, Crossed: This stitch is used for still more decorative borders and hems than the previous stitch. Work the stitch the same as for blanket stitch but cross each pair of stitches.

Chain Stitch: This stitch is used for lines and for outlines. Worked in close rows it is also used for a filling stitch. The stitches are worked from the top down. Bring needle to right side of fabric. Hold thread down with left thumb. Insert needle back where thread emerges. Bring out a short distance away. Draw out needle over loop.

Chain Stitch Band, Raised: This stitch is used for borders. First work a foundation of straight stitches spaced evenly apart. Work from the top down over the foundation stitches and do not pick up fabric. Bring needle up just above first foundation stitch; pass needle over and under this stitch, bring out toward left; then make a stitch as shown in diagram. Pass needle over and under next foundation stitch and repeat.

Chain Stitch, Broad: This stitch is used for lines, borders and stems. Work from top down. Bring needle up at top of line. Make a small straight stitch and bring needle out below. Pass needle back under straight stitch without picking up fabric; insert in same place it last emerged; bring out below. Make stitches in same manner, passing needle back under last chain stitch made.

Chain Stitch, Cable: This is just an interesting variation of the Chain Stitch and serves the same purposes. Bring needle up at top of line to be covered. Holding thread down with left thumb, pass needle from right to left under thread held down; twist needle into vertical position, thread twisted around it. Insert in fabric the desired length and draw it through over working thread.

Chain Stitch, Zigzag Cable: This is a simple variation of the preceding stitch. Work the same as Chain Stitch, Cable but make each stitch at right angles to the last stitch.

Chain Stitch, Checkered: This stitch is sometimes called a Magic Chain since one of the colors disappears each time a stitch is taken. Use it as you would any chain stitch but for especially decorative effects. Thread a needle with 2 colors of thread. Work as a regular chain stitch but when you are ready to pull the needle through, place dark thread over the needle and draw needle through over the light thread. Reverse for next stitch.

Chain Stitch, Double: This stitch is used for wide borders. Work from the top down. Bring needle up at A; insert at B and bring out at C. Place the thread over to the left and insert needle at A; bring out at D and work a similar stitch. Then insert needle at C and work a similar stitch. For fourth stitch, insert needle in second stitch. Alternate stitches in this manner.

Chain Stitch, Heavy: This stitch is used for wide lines, borders and broad stems. Work from top down. Make a small running stitch at top of line to be covered. Bring needle out a little below this stitch; thread under running stitch; insert needle in fabric where it last emerged. Bring out below this point and thread it again under running stitch; take it back into fabric where it last emerged. Each chain is made by working back under the 2 previous loops.

Chain Stitch, Knotted: This stitch is used for lines. Work from right to left. Bring needle up at end of line. Make a small vertical stitch on the line toward the left (a slightly slanted stitch is formed). Hold working thread down with left thumb; slip needle under slanted stitch from top to bottom (do not pick up fabric); pull thread through until a loop is formed; pass needle through this loop; pull thread away and toward the left.

Chain Stitch, Open: This stitch has many names— Roman Chain, Ladder Stitch, Broad Chain. Whatever you call it, it is used for borders, wide lines and even for casings through which a ribbon may be run. Work from the top down. Bring needle out at A. Hold thread down with left thumb; insert needle at B, bring out a little below A, draw thread through over working thread. Leave loop just formed a little loose as next stitch is inserted in it. Work next stitch as shown in diagram.

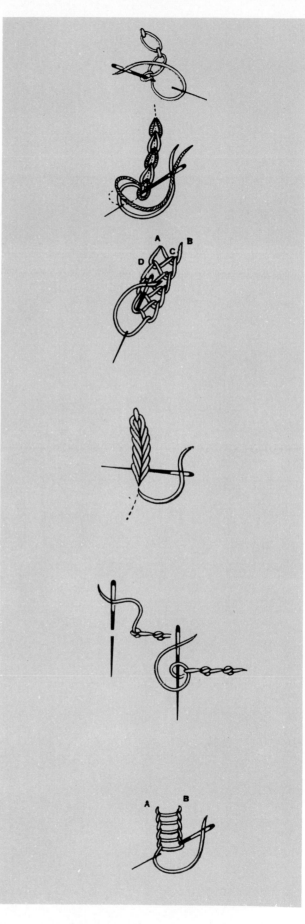

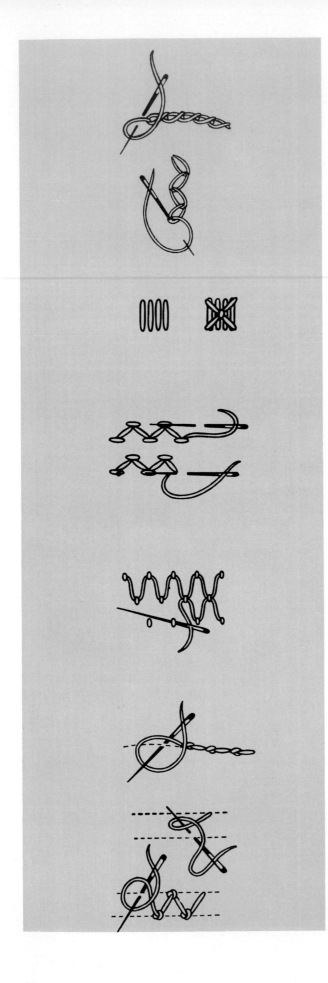

Chain Stitch, Twisted: Use this stitch for lines and borders. Work from right to left. Work as chain stitch but take a slanting stitch as shown and do not work back in previous stitch.

Chain Stitch, Zigzag: This is still another decorative variation of Chain Stitch. Work from top down. Work as for chain stitch but make each loop at an angle to the preceding loop. Run the needle through the thread of the preceding loop each time so that the stitch will lie flat.

Chessboard Filling: This stitch is used for light filling in fairly large areas. Make groups of 4 satin stitches (slightly spaced or close together). Make a cross-stitch over each group, then make a small stitch in the center where stitches cross.

Chevron Stitch: This stitch is used for lines, borders and, when rows are combined, for filling. Work from left to right. Bring needle up on lower line, insert needle to the right and bring out in the center of the stitch being formed. Make a stitch to the right on top line (first step in diagram). Then still on the top line, insert needle to the right and bring out in the center of the stitch now being formed. This step is similar to that shown in the lower half of the diagram. Continue in this manner on lower line then on top line.

Cloud Filling Stitch: This stitch is used for filling large areas. Make a foundation of rows of tiny stitches as shown. Lace through these stitches (in another color if desired) first on the top row, then the row just below, alternating to the end of the row. On the next row lace stitches so loops meet under the same stitch as shown.

Coral Stitch: This stitch is used for lines, for outlines and sometimes as filling. Work from right to left. Bring needle up at end of line to be embroidered. Hold down thread with left thumb, then make a tiny slanting stitch across line. Draw needle under and over thread as shown.

Coral Stitch, Zigzag: This stitch is used for borders. Work the same as coral stitch but alternate stitches on an upper and lower line. Work over loops of thread as shown.

Couching Stitch: This stitch is used for outlines and lines. Place one or more threads along line to be covered, fastening them on the back at the right end of line and holding them with the left thumb as you work. With another thread, work small evenly-spaced stitches over these threads to hold them in place. At end of row draw all threads to back of work and fasten off.

Couching Stitch, Bokhara: This stitch is used for a solid filling. It is worked the same as couching but the same thread is used for the ground and the tying-down stitches. Carry thread from left to right across space to be filled; then work back as shown, making small slanting stitches at even intervals over this thread. The tying-down stitches should be rather close together and pulled tight.

Couching Stitch, Rumanian: This stitch is worked the same as Bokhara Couching but when you are working back over the thread, make the stitches longer and more slanted.

Cretan Stitch, Open: This stitch is used for lines, borders or filling. Work from left to right. Bring needle up on lower line. Make a small vertical stitch on top line as shown. Then with needle pointing up, make a similar stitch on lower line.

Cretan Stitch Leaf: This stitch is worked from the top down. Bring thread out at A. Make a small stitch B-C, drawing needle out over the loop of thread. Now make stitch D-E, again drawing needle out over the loop. Continue making stitches first one side then the other, adjusting the length of stitch to the outline. Note how decoratively the stitches interlock in the center.

Cross-stitch: This stitch is usually worked on crosses already transferred to fabric or on fabric which has threads that can be counted easily. Starting at lower left corner of a stitch and working from left to right, make a diagonal stitch (half cross-stitch) to upper right corner. Continue across, making a row of slanting stitches each going over an equal number of threads or over transferred pattern. Work back over these stitches as shown. You can work each cross-stitch individually and in any direction but they must all cross in the same direction.

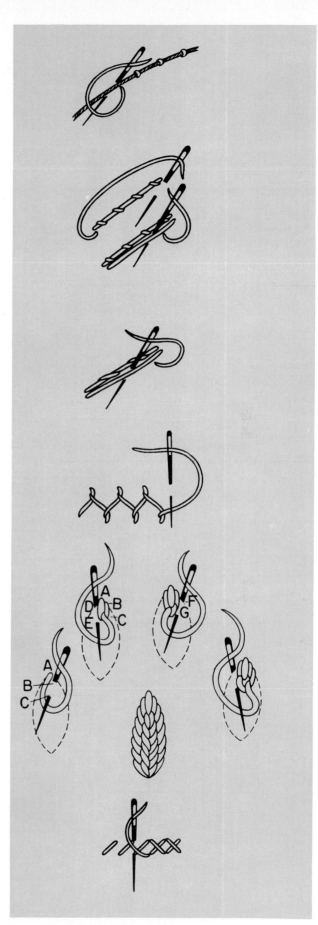

Diamond Stitch: This stitch is used for borders. Work from the top down. Bring needle up on left line. Insert on right line and bring up directly below. Hold thread toward left; pass needle under the 2 threads as shown; draw needle through over working thread (knot made on right side of first stitch). Make a similar knot on left side of same stitch. Insert the needle in the left line right next to the knot just made; bring out below. Make a knot in the center on the lower of the 2 horizontal stitches. Make a stitch on the right line; make a knot, then make a knot on the left. Insert needle next to knot just made, bring out below. Then make a knot in the center.

Ermine Filling Stitch: This stitch is used for a spaced filling or for a border when worked in a row. Make a long straight stitch for center, then work an elongated cross-stitch over center stitch.

Eyelet Hole: This stitch is used in cutwork and eyelet embroidery. Draw circle of desired size on fabric. Work running stitches around it. Cut out center. Overcast all around circle, working over the running stitches.

Feather Stitch: This stitch is used for lines, borders, outlines, fern-like leaves and light filling. Work from top to bottom. Bring needle up a little to left of line to be covered. Hold thread down with left thumb; make a slanting stitch to the right and a little below this spot with needle pointing to the left; draw needle through over working thread. Carry thread to left side of line to be covered and make a similar stitch a little below this spot with needle pointing to the right; draw needle through over working thread.

Feather Stitch, Closed: This stitch is used for borders and wide lines. Work from the top down. Bring needle up at A; insert at B and bring out a little below. Note that needle is held perpendicularly on this and all subsequent stitches. Draw through over working thread. Insert needle just below starting point and make a similar stitch on left side (just like stitch being worked on diagram). Repeat, making stitches on right side then on left. Make stitches close together so that an almost unbroken line is formed at outer edges.

Feather Stitch, Long-Armed: This stitch is used for borders and filling. Work from the top down. Bring needle up at top of line to be covered. Insert to left and a little lower down; bring out at center; draw needle through over working thread. Make a similar stitch to right. Continue, alternating stitches.

Feather Stitch, Single: This stitch is used for lines, irregular outlines and smocking. Work from the top down. Bring needle up at top of line to be covered. Hold thread down with left thumb. Make a slanting stitch as shown and draw needle through over working thread. Repeat stitch on same side throughout.

Fern Stitch: This stitch is used for leaf veins or fern-like leaves. Work 3 straight stitches all radiating from the same center hole. Continue on so that the center stitches of each group form a continuous line.

Fishbone Stitch: This stitch is used to cover an entire area. Make a short stitch at top of area to be filled. Bring needle up on left edge; insert it a little below first stitch and just across center line; bring out on right edge. Make a similar stitch inserting needle to left of center line and bringing it out at left edge. Each succeeding stitch should slant and cross at the center.

Fishbone Stitch, Raised: This stitch, when finished, looks just like the preceding one but looks thicker and more cushiony. Make 3 stitches at top of area to be filled, ending with thread coming from left edge as shown in upper diagram. Insert needle on right edge, bring out on left edge directly opposite. Insert needle on right edge just below lowest stitch as shown in lower diagram; bring out needle on left edge directly opposite. Repeat these 2 steps shown in upper and lower diagrams.

Fly Stitch: This stitch is used for a light filling or, when worked in a row, for borders. Bring thread up at upper left corner of stitch; insert needle directly opposite (upper right corner of stitch) and bring out in center below; draw through over working thread. Make a small stitch to tie down loop. This tying-down stitch can be made various lengths for different effects.

French Knot: This stitch is used in groups for flower centers, for light filling and where the effect of a single dot is required. The thread is often used double or triple for a bigger dot. Bring needle up where dot is to be made. Wind thread 2 or 3 times around point of needle, insert in fabric as close as possible to spot where thread emerged (but not in exact spot) and pull to wrong side, holding twists of stitch in place.

Herringbone Stitch: This stitch is used for borders, wide lines and as a foundation for other stitches. Work from left to right. Bring needle up at A; insert at B, bring out at C; then insert at D, bring out at E. Continue in this manner.

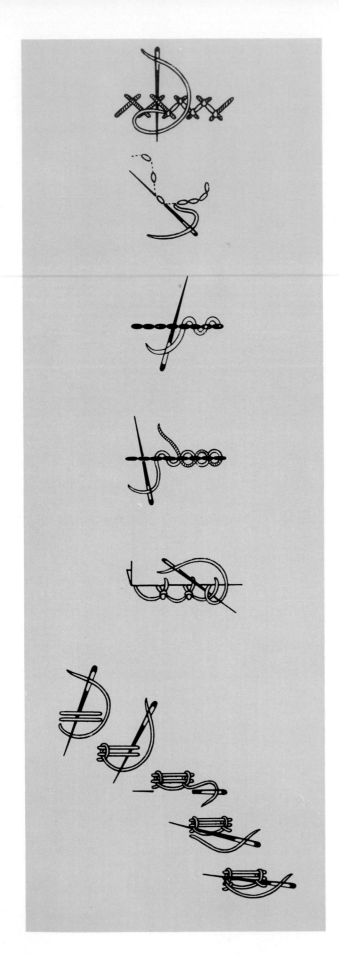

Herringbone Stitch, Tied: This is a more decorative version of herringbone and is used for borders. Make a foundation of herringbone stitches. Then work coral stitch over them, making a knot over intersections without picking up fabric.

Holbein Stitch: This stitch is used for lines and outlines. It is often used to outline solid areas of cross-stitch. Work running stitch along line to be covered, making sure that each stitch and space between stitches are all of equal size. Then work running stitch back over this line, filling in the empty spaces.

Holbein Stitch, Single-Threaded: This stitch is used for special emphasis on lines and borders. Work a foundation of Holbein Stitch. Then thread another color or weight of yarn through these stitches, not carrying it to back of fabric at all. Sometimes it is easier to insert the *eye* of the needle under the stitch rather than the point. Threading can be tight or loose depending on the effect you want.

Holbein Stitch, Double-Threaded: Complete the first 2 steps of Holbein Stitch, Single-Threaded. Then with thread of the same color as the first threading, (or a contrasting color), work back over the line of stitches to make loops on the opposite side of stitches.

Knot Stitch: This stitch is used to trim a hem or a turned-over edge. Work from left to right. Bring needle to right side at fold. With needle in vertical position, insert needle to right through hem and bring out below hem over working thread (do not pull tightly). Take another stitch over this loop as shown and pull into a knot.

Ladder Stitch: This stitch is used for wide borders and for filling. The sides are usually straight but an interesting effect can be achieved by expanding the width of the ladder as you work. Work from the top down. Make 2 horizontal stitches the desired width. Then pass needle under these horizontal stitches as shown. Do not pick up fabric. Make a similar loop stitch on right side (2nd step in diagram). Then insert needle in right edge; bring out on left edge (3rd step). Insert needle between 2nd and 3rd rungs of ladder, pass it under both threads of left-hand loop, draw through without picking up fabric (4th step). Work under right-hand loop in same manner (5th step). Repeat steps 3, 4 and 5. Pull thread slightly to the left after making left-hand loops but leave it a little loose when making right-hand loops. This will keep stitches even.

Laid Stitch: This stitch looks just like satin stitch but requires less thread and is somewhat flatter. Make a stitch like a satin stitch across area to be filled. Do not return to starting edge but make next stitch as shown, leaving size of a stitch between the two. Work all across the area then fill open spaces with another series of stitches.

Laid Work, Tied: This stitch is used for solid and very decorative filling. First fill in entire area to be worked in laid stitch. Then make a series of diagonal stitches over the laid stitch. Make another series of diagonal stitches crossing the first diagonal stitches at right angles. Tie down the diagonal stitches at intersections with a series of little stitches, as lower diagram. The laid stitches, the diagonal stitches and the tying down stitches may all be worked in different colors.

Lazy-daisy Stitch: This stitch is used for flowers and light filling. Bring thread up in center of "flower". Hold thread down with left thumb; insert needle close to or in exact spot where thread emerged and bring out desired distance (the length of the petal — see upper figure in diagram). Draw through over working thread. Then tie down with a tiny stitch made over loop as shown. Make similar stitches to form a circle around same center point. Diagram shows them slightly separated for clarity, but they can be made in same center hole.

Lazy-daisy Stitch, Long-tailed: This stitch is a simple variation of Lazy-daisy Stitch. It is worked in the same manner as the Lazy-daisy but the loop is smaller and the tying-down stitch is longer and is made toward the center.

Long and Short Stitch: This stitch is used for filling and for shading. Work the same as Satin Stitch, except that you stagger long and short stitches over the area to be covered. The irregular line makes a very softly shaded effect when closely related colors are used.

Long and Short Stitch, Surface: This stitch is used to save thread. It is worked the same as Long and Short Stitch but the Satin Stitches are worked on the surface (see Satin Stitch, Surface). The needle does not travel so far underneath the fabric.

Outline Stitch: This stitch is used for outlines, stems and any fine lines. Bring needle up at left end of line. Working from left to right, insert needle a short distance to the right and bring out a little way to the left at a very slight angle. Keep thread above the needle. **Note:** If thread is held below the needle, the stitch is known as Stem, or Crewel Stitch.

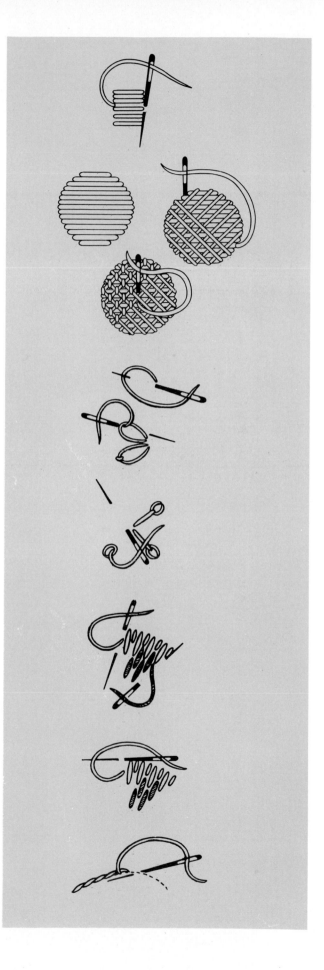

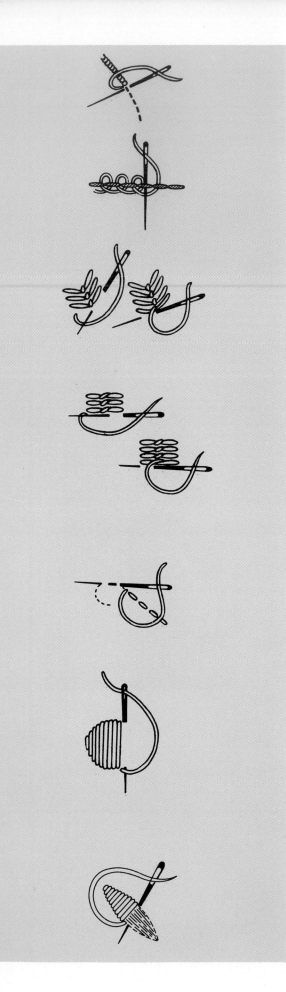

Overcast Stitch: This stitch is used for stems, outlines and monogramming. Work a row of running stitches along line to be covered. Then work small close stitches across these stitches. Pick up the smallest amount of fabric possible.

Pekingese Stitch: This stitch is used for borders. First make a row of backstitches. Without picking up fabric, lace second thread (in another color, if desired) through these stitches.

Roman Stitch: This stitch is used for borders or filling. Work from the top down. Bring needle up on left line; insert exactly opposite on right line; bring out in center. Then make a tiny stitch over this loop and bring needle out on left line (second step in diagram). Stitches can be made slightly curved as shown or perfectly straight.

Rumanian Stitch: This stitch is used for borders or filling. Work from the top down. Bring needle up on left line; insert exactly opposite on right line; bring it out about halfway back toward left line, draw through over working thread. Then tie this stitch down with a slanting stitch as shown.

Running Stitch: This stitch may be worked on a straight or curved line. It is used for outlines, a foundation for other stitches and for filling when worked in close rows. Work from right to left and make stitches even in size and evenly spaced. If work is in a hoop, only one stitch can be made at a time. If work is in the hand, 2 or 3 stitches can be made at a time. Running stitch may be threaded with another color (see Holbein Stitch, Single-Threaded or Holbein Stitch, Double-Threaded).

Satin Stitch: This stitch is used where background fabric is to be covered completely but over an area that is not too large. Bring needle up at one edge of area to be covered, insert at opposite edge and return to starting edge by carrying it underneath fabric. Stitches may be vertical, horizontal or diagonal but should always be parallel and close together.

Satin Stitch, Padded: For a slightly raised effect pad the area with stitches before working satin stitch. Straight stitches are used here. Padding may also be chain stitch or satin stitch. In any case, the padding is usually worked in the opposite direction to the final satin stitch.

Satin Stitch, Surface: This stitch is used to save thread. It is worked the same as Satin Stitch but the needle does not go all the way underneath area to be covered. Take a tiny stitch at the edge, then take a tiny stitch at opposite edge. For a closer alignment of stitches, however, use Laid Stitch.

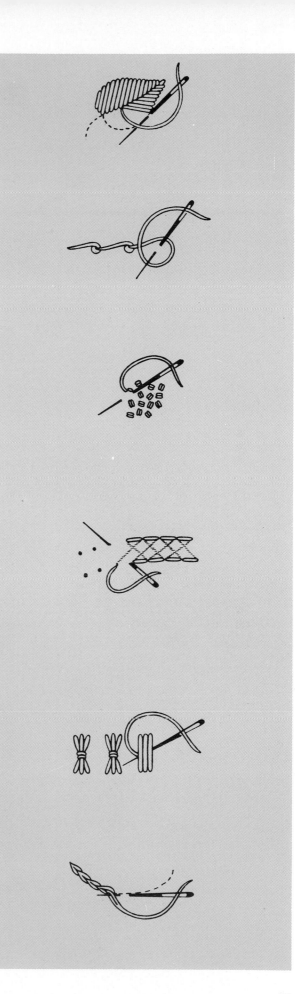

Scroll Stitch: This stitch is used for borders. Work from left to right. Bring needle up at end of line to be covered. Make a loop of thread as shown. Insert needle in center of loop across line to be covered and pick up a small amount of fabric; pull loop tightly under point of needle, then draw needle through.

Seed Stitch: This stitch (sometimes called Seeding Stitch) is used for light filling and may be as dense as shown or more widely scattered. Make tiny straight stitches in any direction. The stitches are not worked in a regular pattern but should be of equal length. They can be made single or double as shown.

Shadow Stitch: This stitch is worked on sheer fabric so that the under part of the stitch shows through in a shadow effect. Work from right to left. Make a small backstitch on one side of area to be filled, slant needle to other side of space, make another backstitch. Shadow Stitch is worked on right side of fabric but main part of stitch appears on wrong side so that X's show through fabric while rows of continuous backstitches are on right side. This stitch may be worked across a variety of shapes — a leaf, a flower or a circle, for instance. The X's will vary in size but the backstitches will always be of equal size.

Sheaf Filling Stitch: This stitch is used for filling. Make 3 vertical satin stitches. Then bring needle out at center of left side; wrap thread around center twice without picking up fabric and insert where thread emerged.

Split Stitch: This stitch is used for outlines, stems and fine lines. When worked in close rows, it is used for filling. Close rows worked in closely related colors produce shading for leaves and flowers. Work split stitch like stem stitch (see Outline Stitch), then split working thread close to its base when you bring needle out.

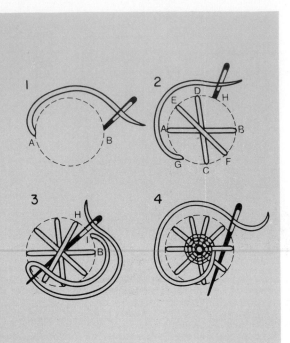

Spider Web, Whipped: This stitch is used as a highly decorative spot such as the center of a large flower. If your fabric is not too tightly woven, use a tapestry needle. Bring thread out at A; insert needle at B (diagram 1). Then bring needle out at C; insert at D (note that C-D is slightly off the true vertical). Bring needle out at E; insert at F; bring out at G; insert at H (note in diagram 2 that H is closer to D than to B). Bring needle out at I (halfway between H and B). Without inserting needle in fabric, run it under all the threads at the center; loop thread over needle as shown (diagram 3); pull needle through and pull upwards, knotting threads together in center. Continuing with the same working thread, run needle under 2 threads at the center; then run needle under the last thread used and 1 new thread (diagram 4). Repeat this process, going back over 1 thread and running needle under 2 threads, until the spokes are all covered. If desired, edge of Spider Web can be outlined with any basic stitch suggested for outlines.

Spider Web, Woven: This stitch is a slightly different version of Spider Web. Follow diagrams 1, 2 and 3 in preceding directions. When the spokes have been knotted together at center, continue on with same working thread. Weave under 1 spoke, over 1 spoke until entire web is filled. If desired, edge of Spider Web can be outlined with any basic stitch suggested for outlines.

Star Filling Stitch: This stitch is used for rather open filling of an area or combined with other stitches. Work a cross-stitch on the straight rather than the diagonal. Then work another cross-stitch of equal size right over the first one, this time placing it on the diagonal. Finally, work a tiny cross-stitch in the center over the intersection of the first two.

Straight Stitch: This stitch is used as an occasional single stitch scattered in a design or grouped in a ring to form a flower. Each stitch is always separated from the next one.

Thorn Stitch: This stitch is used for stems and leaves. First make a long center stitch from bottom of line to the top. Then work diagonal stitches over the center stitch from the top down.

Trellis Stitch: This stitch is used for filling especially where a lattice effect is desired. It is often used on flower centers. Work long horizontal stitches evenly spaced across area to be filled. Then work long vertical stitches across these. Work a cross-stitch, (sometimes only a half cross-stitch) at each intersection. A different weight or color of thread may be used to work cross-stitches.

Vandyke Stitch: This stitch is used for borders. Bring needle up at 1. Insert at 2 and bring out at 3. Then insert at 4 and bring out at 5. For next stitch insert needle under center crossed stitches and without picking up fabric draw needle through. Insert needle in right edge below last stitch, bring out directly below last stitch on left edge.

Wave Stitch, Open: This stitch is used for filling. Work a row of small straight vertical stitches from left to right across top of area to be filled (shaded stitches on diagram). Bring needle up on right edge below these stitches. Slip needle under first straight stitch and without picking up fabric, draw needle through. Make a tiny horizontal stitch below and on line with point where thread last emerged; then work under next straight stitch. The third and all following rows are slipped under the bases of 2 stitches of the previous row as shown.

Wheat-ear Stitch: This stitch is used for stems, borders and wheatlike stalks. Work from top down. Bring needle up on line to be covered (1); insert at 2; bring out at 3. Insert close to spot where thread first emerged and bring out a distance below. Then without picking up fabric, slip needle from right to left underneath the first 2 stitches (upper diagram). Insert needle in spot where thread last emerged and bring out to left as shown in lower diagram. Insert needle in bottom of loop and bring out above and to the right; insert again at bottom of loop and bring out a distance below.

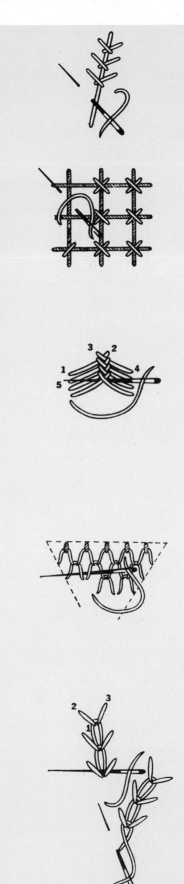

Hardanger

Hardanger is the first of the next three needle-work techniques which we shall call "white work." Although it is possible to carry them out in colored threads on colored backgrounds, they are traditionally worked in white (or off-white) threads on a white (or natural-color) background. Their charm lies in the subtle play of perfect stitches against a pristine background. Most often these techniques are used to embellish household linens. Their very elegance makes them ideal wedding gifts, sure to become treasured heirlooms.

Hardanger (pronounced "hardonger" by the needlework cognoscenti) is known essentially as Scandinavian embroidery. Actually, the technique was developed in Asia long before it was worked in the northern countries and named for the province of Hardanger in Norway.

MATERIALS

A background fabric of an even weave is essential. Hardanger cloth, 42"-inch wide cotton, is available in a few needlework shops. The weave of this is very easy to count. If you cannot find this, use regular even-weave linen. Generally a linen or twisted cotton embroidery thread is used. (Never use 6-strand floss.) The thread is usually just a little heavier than the background fabric, although occasionally the blocks may be worked in one weight of thread and other stitch details may be developed in a lighter weight thread.

EQUIPMENT

A large hoop is needed. A blunt tapestry needle will separate the threads of the background fabric properly, although if you should be using very fine linen, you may have to switch to a crewel needle. Hardanger is one form of needlework for which an embroidery scissors is essential.

METHOD

The work is made up of satin stitch blocks, called klosters, which often outline cutout squares. These squares are sometimes ornamented with additional stitches. To learn hardanger, put a piece of fabric in a hoop and practice making klosters as follows:

START

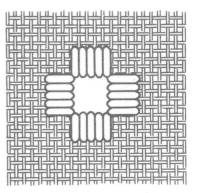

Working over 4 threads, make 5 vertical satin stitches right to left as in diagram. Come out at A and change direction by working 5 horizontal stitches. Note that point A is the corner of 2 adjoining klosters. Continue around in this manner until the square is finished. Now cut out the center of the square carefully. **Note:** Never cut out a square first and then try to work the satin stitches over it. Further variations of hardanger are developed in the project which follows these general directions.

HARDANGER TABLECLOTH

Although making this tablecloth will give you the reputation of being a needlework expert, it is relatively easy to embroider. The design is concentrated in the center of the cloth so that is will not conflict with the placing of your best crystal and silver. The little motifs are so versatile, however, that they can be adapted to a wide or narrow border and to napkins in a great variety of ways.

HARDANGER TABLECLOTH

SIZE: About 54″ square.

MATERIALS: 1½ yards 54″ natural-color even-weave linen; pearl cotton, size 5, 4 balls ecru; sewing thread.

EQUIPMENT: Embroidery hoop; fine tapestry needle; embroidery scissors.

PREPARATION: Even up fabric by pulling threads and cutting straight edges. Overcast edges to prevent fraying. Mark exact center of cloth, both vertically and horizontally, with a basting thread of a bright color. Put center area in hoop.

EMBROIDERY: Note: Work all embroidery on cloth before cutting out any squares. If you have to move hoop over any embroidered areas, protect them with tissue paper. Follow detailed photograph for motifs. Work first motif (1) in very center of cloth. Add 8 more of these motifs around center motif, placing them just 2 threads from each other at outer points. Leave 8 threads plain around motifs, then work border (2). Leave 8 threads plain around border and work 2 motifs (3) on each side, placing them 3 threads beyond center basting lines. Work crosses (4) and corner motifs (5). Seven threads beyond edge of motifs (3), work border (6). Remove from hoop and cut out centers of border squares.

FINISHING: Hem tablecloth following directions for mitering corners (see Index).

Hemstitching

Fine needlework deserves a handsome finish and one of the most elegant ways to hem table linens, guest towels, most household linens in fact, is by hemstitching. Hemstitching can be so lovely that— in its more elaborate forms—it may provide the only decoration on such items as napkins and pillow cases.

Hemstitching is a method by which the hem is often sewn in place at the same time that a decorative border is worked. This border usually consists of one or more bands of drawn threads. The remaining threads are then drawn into neat little groups. Although drawn thread work is an entire category of needlework, only plain hemstitching, Italian hemstitching and simple crossed cluster hemstitching are given here. Perfect these stitches, combine them and you will be able to produce handsome borders.

MATERIALS

Almost any fabric of a plain weave can be hemstitched. You will find it easier to work on fabric in which the threads are all of the same thickness, however. Although very fine fabric—such as handkerchief linen—can be hemstitched, it is advisable for the beginner to work on cotton or linen in which one can see and count the threads easily.

Although the origins of hemstitching are lost in antiquity, it is known that the earliest pieces were worked with the actual threads drawn from the background fabric. You can try this method just so that you can tell your friends that you do your hemstitching the way it was done in biblical times. However you will find it more practical to use a good quality sewing thread—preferably linen—for hemstitching. Generally the working thread should be approximately the same weight as a thread of the background fabric. Occasionally a slightly heavier thread is introduced in the detailed stitches (such as the crossed cluster stitch shown in this section). Hemstitching may be worked with a colored thread on a natural-color linen but almost all hemstitching is worked with a thread of the same color as the background fabric—or just a shade darker.

EQUIPMENT

Since hemstitching is worked in the hand, no hoop or frame is needed. Use a fine tapestry needle so that you can separate the background threads easily.

METHOD

First true up your piece of fabric by pulling out a thread, then cutting the edges on the straight of the goods. To pull out a thread: lift one thread with the point of a pin so that you have an end to hold, then draw the thread out carefully.

Although hemstitching may be purely decorative, it usually also serves the purpose of holding the hem in place as well. Turn raw edge to wrong side, then turn hem of the desired width to wrong side following exact thread of the fabric; baste. **Note:** If you are hemstitching a napkin or tablecloth, see Index for directions for mitering corners.

Plain Hemstitching: Decide how much open work you want and draw out the number of threads necessary (2, 3 or more) just beyond the hem. **Note:** Generally threads are not pulled across hems at sides of work. To prevent this, the designer of the needlework in this book adapted a most ingenious way to draw the threads out and yet have nice neat edges next to the side hems. It is not usually done on this type of needlework but since it eliminates the cut threads and possible fraying at the sides we recommend it highly.

Clip the thread to be drawn in the **center** of the row. With a pin draw out the thread as far as the side hem. Do not cut off. Repeat with other half of thread, drawing it to opposite side hem. Insert a pin in each side hem and wrap the loose threads around pins. When hemstitching is completed, insert each loose thread in a needle and work back into hem, then clip off excess.

There are many ways to do plain hemstitching. The diagram shows just one method. It is usually worked on the wrong side and from left to right. Hide end of thread in the hem and fasten with a few little stitches. Bring needle up a little below drawn thread section, catching about 2 threads of hem. (The hem does not show in the diagram.) Put needle from right to left under desired number (2, 3, 4) vertical threads in the drawn thread section. Draw thread up tight. Then insert needle into hem section. Alternate these two steps across row. Other edge of drawn thread section may also be hemstitched if desired.

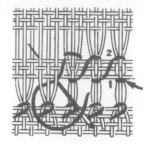

Italian Hemstitching: For a more elaborate border draw out 2 or 3 threads beyond your basted hem. Skip 3 threads, then draw out the same number of threads as before. To fasten hem, work plain hemstitching picking up 3 threads in each little group.

Now fasten working thread at right side of the drawn thread section (arrow in diagram). Working from right to left, bring needle up at 1 and insert back at arrow. Bring needle up at 2 and go around the same 3 threads in upper drawn thread section. Then continue stitch back to lower drawn thread section. Continue across row. **Note 1:** Keep each little group of threads in line with those on first row of hemstitching. **Note 2:** Top edge of upper drawn thread section may also be hemstitched if desired.

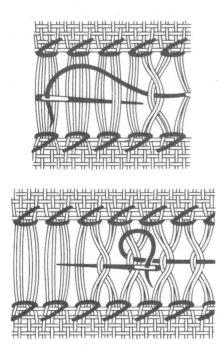

Crossed Cluster Hemstitching: For a really impressive border which is quick to make try this stitch. Beyond basted hem draw out a wide area of threads (8, 9, 10 or desired number). Work plain hemstitching at each edge of drawn thread section, making little groups of 4 threads. Be sure that these little groups line up at top and bottom of drawn thread section.

Now on **right side** of work fasten thread at right-hand side in middle of drawn thread section. Also fasten down 2 threads of first group in the same place. Pick up 2 threads of second group (see diagram A) with needle pointing from left to right. Pull this group of threads over and to the right of the remaining 2 threads of the first group and, with needle pointing from right to left, scoop up the remaining 2 threads of the first group (see diagram B). Continue across row.

All pieces began with a ¼" hem held in place with plain hemstitching.

1. In this example 3 threads were drawn beyond the hem. Plain hemstitching was worked tightly on the bottom and top of the drawn thread section to produce the straight neat groups.

2. This is an example of hemstitching where *no* threads have been drawn. Two bands of Italian hemstitching were worked over 3 horizontal threads each. The stitches were pulled up rather tightly to produce the little openings.

3. This example had 1 thread drawn beyond hem, 3 threads were skipped, then 1 more thread was drawn. Italian hemstitching was worked over the 3-thread area.

4. This example is standard crossed cluster hemstitching worked over a 6-drawn thread section. **Note:** In the photograph the crossings seem to go in the opposite direction to those in the diagrams for this stitch. Actually the sample was worked exactly as the stitch in the diagrams but the work happened to be held with the hem above the drawn threads rather than below.

If hemstitching appeals to you, don't limit yourself to just decorating guest towels. Design 1 shown opposite would be handsome as a border on each side of the buttonhole section of a dainty blouse; design 2 would be charming on a crisp linen collar; 3 could edge a deep hem on a little girl's dress; 4 would be great worked in color on a tote bag.

Monogramming

Perhaps the most personal gift imaginable is one bearing a monogram. It can never have been meant for anyone except the recipient. If it is a handmade gift, it indicates just that much more that it was lovingly worked for no one else in the world. If you want to make a gift demonstrating your sincere affection or true love, none will express it better than one with a monogram.

In a more leisurely era, a girl marked every item in her trousseau with an elaborate cipher of initials. A woman replaced every worn sheet, even kitchen towels, with one marked with a carefully worked monogram. She also marked her own lingerie, her husband's shirts, even her children's clothing with an appropriate monogram. Today laundry marks and camp labels take care of the identification. We enjoy our monograms purely as decoration.

There are commercial transfers available for many kinds of initials. Or you can easily find interesting letters in magazines and newspapers. To give you some useful background in working monograms, however, we shall present some basic information here and complete sets of initials for you to use as shown or to adapt to your needs.

THE ETIQUETTE OF MONOGRAMS

For men: If the letters are to be all the same size, use his first initial, middle initial, last initial—in that order. If you want a large center letter flanked by two smaller ones in your design, use his first initial, last initial, middle initial—in that order.

For women: The rules for men's monograms apply to unmarried women as well. The married woman replaces her middle initial with that of her maiden name. If she was Mary Jane Smith and married Mr. Brown, her new monogram is MSB if the letters are all one size. If there is to be a larger center letter, her monogram is MBS.

Placement of monograms is generally a matter of good common sense. Obviously you would not monogram a sheet on a corner which will be tucked under the mattress. Sheets are monogrammed in the center just above the top hem so that the monogram falls in the right position when the sheet is turned down over the blanket. Pillow cases are usually monogrammed in the center just above the hem.

Tablecloths may be marked at one end (or both ends if the cloth is large) in the right-hand corner. Or the monogram may be centered at each end just above the area of the place settings. Table mats are marked on the left side either vertically or horizontally (near the top). Napkins are usually monogrammed in one corner in a style similar to that used on the cloth or mat but on a smaller scale.

METHOD

Trace the initials desired from the alphabet shown. Letters are about 1″. If you want larger letters, enlarge them in the usual way. If more elaborate letters are desired, add the curlicues as on the S or the HJ in the photographs. Or you might frame the letters like the sample S or the towels marked

G and IU. Note how the addition of an embroidered dot enlivens the J and the design of LO.

When you have worked out your entire design on paper, transfer it to your project. Place work in an embroidery hoop. Monograms shown were all worked with 4 strands of 6-strand floss. Satin stitch is used most often for monogramming. For a luxurious quality to the letters the satin stitch is usually padded. (For all stitches see the Index). Split stitch or chain stitch can also be used for the padding. Work the padding with a slightly heavier thread than the satin stitch.

For informal monograms, many different stitches may be used. The sample letter S was worked in Holbein stitch with a scattering of French knots. The frame circling it consists of 2 lines of chain stitch separated by a line of Holbein. The sample letters HJ were worked in Holbein stitch with a trim of French knots.

The towel marked IU has satin stitch letters outlined with Holbein stitch. The interlocking circles are coral stitch. The letters LO are chain stitch with a trim of French knots. The letter G is all chain stitch. Its frame consists of a ring of chain edged with rings of Holbein. The scallops are Holbein.

Occasionally we'd like a monogram on a garment or a heavy bath towel that doesn't lend itself to embroidery. A sweater is a good example. To embroider on knit goods first apply monogram design to a firm lightweight fabric—organdy, muslin or the like—cut large enough to fit in your embroidery hoop. Baste this fabric to your sweater exactly where you want the decoration to be, making sure that you do not stretch the knitting. Place work in hoop. Embroider the monogram then carefully cut away the extra fabric so that only the monogram remains.

Just a reminder: Cross-stitch monograms can be handsome too. They are particularly appropriate on children's garments and informal household linens. Don't forget there is a complete alphabet on the sampler in the cross-stitch section.

Perhaps the precise nature of a monogram does not appeal to you. In that case, try a first name written out in your own handwriting. A child's name in his own wobbly script is delightful worked in chain stitch on a play outfit.

Helpful Hint: Very often a sheet or pillow case or tablecloth wears out long before the monogram which embellishes it. Just cut out the monogram leaving a narrow border around it. The monogram can then be applied (see section on appliqué) to a similar object.

Just for fun we put a simple embroidery motif on a towel in the grouping. You will notice how well it combines with the monogrammed towels. If you want to copy it, here is a full size design to transfer to your towel. Using 3 strands of 6-strand embroidery floss throughout, work as follows: In center alternate straight stitches of rose and blue. Work a ring of medium blue outline stitch, then dotted area in medium blue laid stitch. Work spiky units in straight stitch, the top 3 in medium blue, the lower 2 in dark blue. Work petal areas in Holbein stitch, the inner line in dark blue, the outer 2 in rose.

ACTUAL SIZE

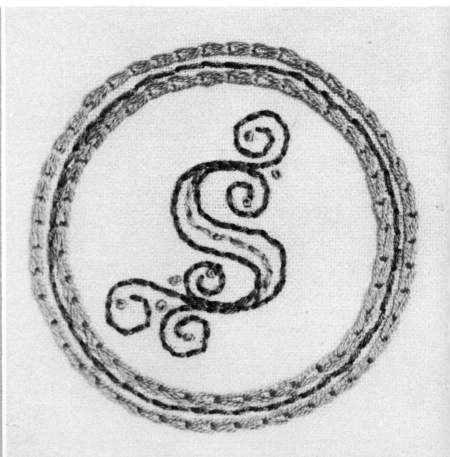

Trace the initials desired from the alphabets shown. They can all be worked in the given size; however, you may want to enlarge yours. To do so, draw in a grid as in the first alphabet. Draw a similar grid to the size you want and copy the letters square for square.

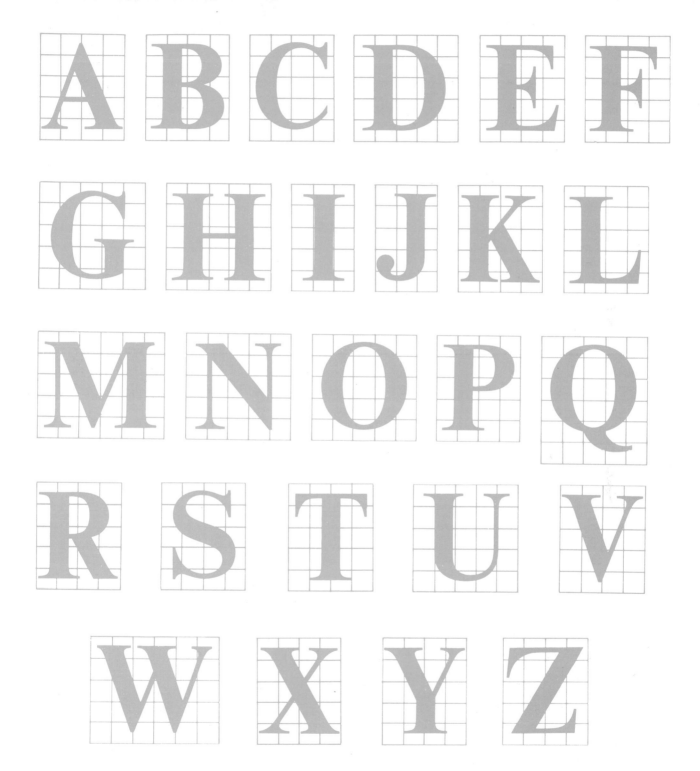

ABCDEF
GHIJKL
MNOPQ
RSTUV
WXYZ123
4567890

aBcdeFG

hijklmn

opqrstu

vwxyz12

34567890

ABCDEF
GHIJKLM
NOPQR
STUVW
XYZ1234
567890

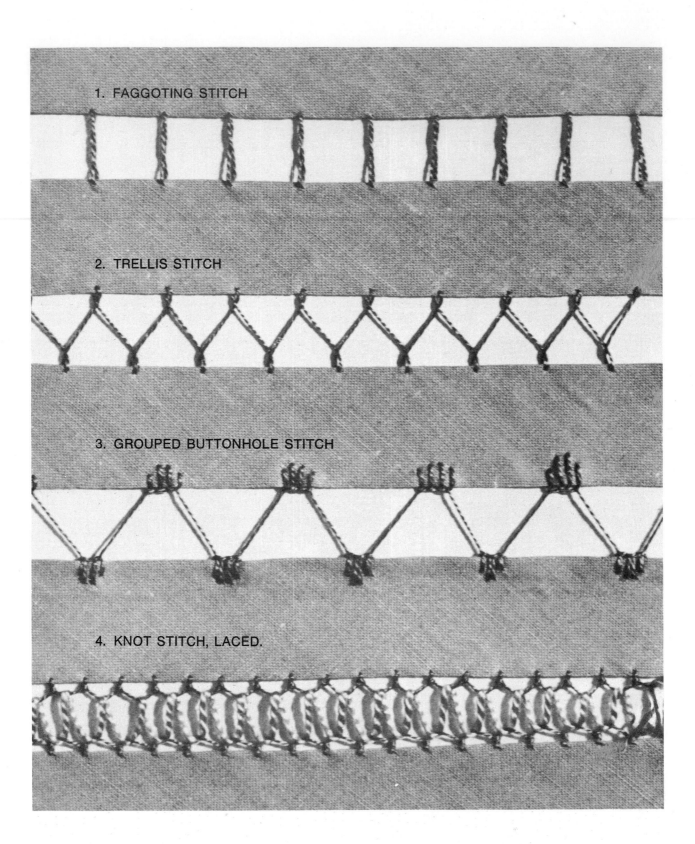

1. FAGGOTING STITCH

2. TRELLIS STITCH

3. GROUPED BUTTONHOLE STITCH

4. KNOT STITCH, LACED.

Faggoting

A charming form of needlework that is due for a revival is faggoting. Quite simply, it is a way of joining two edges, seams or tapes with decorative stitches to form an open lacy pattern. Since it makes use of traditional embroidery stitches, its history is a long and obscure one, but it was last fashionable in the early 1920's—a period which is having a high fashion revival today!

Faggoting can be used on table linens, guest towels and some household items but is even more suitable for clothing. Those of us who make our own clothes rarely take the time to add any fine handwork these days—more's the pity! An extra hour spent in faggoting the center front seam of a linen summer dress would turn it into a couturière's creation. Perhaps we won't attempt the delicate blouses made entirely of satin stripes faggoted together such as our great-aunts made, but we can certainly trim a baby sacque with a bit of lace neatly joined by a row of faggoting.

MATERIALS

Most fabrics can be used for faggoting, but cotton, linen or silk are the most appropriate. Tapes are frequently used as a base and are easy for the beginner to handle. Bias tape of any width is particularly suitable. Many types of cotton, linen or silk embroidery thread can be used but should always be consistent with the fabric background.

EQUIPMENT

A crewel needle of a size to hold your thread is needed. A sewing needle is also basic to the preparation for faggoting. You will need heavy paper large enough to fit the edges you are joining.

METHOD

Prepare the edges of your background fabric by hemming invisibly. If you are using bias tape (or strips of fabric), place wrong sides together, edges turned in, and slip-stitch the edges. Baste the pieces to the heavy paper, leaving ⅛" to ½" between the edges. The width between depends on the weight of the fabric and the object being made but should remain the same throughout any item.

Join the edges with embroidery stitches. In addition to the stitches shown here, the following are also appropriate: Coral Stitch, Zigzag; Braid Stitch on each edge joined with a lacing; Sheaf Stitch. **Note:** All stitches mentioned or shown can be found in the section on embroidery stitches.

To practice faggoting stitches slip-stitch the edges of single-fold bias tape together. Baste lengths of tape to heavy paper, placing them about ½" apart. Usually faggoting is worked closer together but this distance was used for clarity. Use pearl cotton or other embroidery thread. To help you space stitches evenly you may want to make a row of little dots with pencil and ruler on the paper right at the edge of each tape.

Faggoting Stitch: This is one of the basic stitches used in this form of needlework. Work from right to left. Bring thread out at top edge. Bring needle directly across space and insert in lower edge, coming from back to front. Wrap thread around upright bar once, then insert needle in top edge where thread originally came out; slide needle inside top edge to position for next stitch.

A variation of this stitch is made by wrapping the thread around the upright bar as many times as necessary to fill it completely. Continue to next position as before.

Trellis Stitch: This stitch should not be confused with the Trellis Filling Stitch. Follow the directions for the Cretan Stitch, Open.

Grouped Buttonhole Stitch: This is a standard Buttonhole Stitch worked first in one edge, then the other. The number of stitches in a group is optional but should remain the same throughout. In this case 2 longer stitches are worked between 2 shorter ones.

Knot Stitch, Laced: Make a row of Knot Stitch on each edge. With a thread of a heavier weight and/or a contrasting color, lace the 2 rows of stitches together.

Appliqué

If you have ever had a secret yearning to paint a great picture but are sure that you "can't even draw a straight line," appliqué is the needlecraft for you. By sewing bits of fabric to a fabric background—which is just what appliqué is—you will be able to indulge your desire to create objects of real charm that combine many of the elements of fine art. In galleries they call it "collage." We (with the modesty of all needleworkers) simply call it appliqué. Look at the wonderful way you can combine colors—even without the use of a palette. Composition and design? Just move your little snippets of cloth around until you achieve a thoroughly satisfying effect and you become a creator. Texture? Perhaps wool tweed will make that shape look even more like a tree. Suddenly the mere pieces of cloth in your hands become your own contribution to the hand arts.

Although fabric has been applied to a background fabric in a decorative manner wherever fine needlework has been done, appliqué became one of the basic forms of American needlework. When our great-grandmothers finally had the leisure to do something more than the necessary weaving and sewing to keep their families clothed, they looked around for ways to make their simple homes more beautiful. What better way than to embellish the bedcovers that warmed them during the long cold winters? The scraps of calico carefully hoarded from years of dressmaking were used to make gay patterns on their linen and cotton coverlets. Although we may not have the time to produce the dozens of quilts and bedcovers that our ancestors did, we can derive the same pleasure in appliquéing bright pieces of fabric to a cosy sofa cushion or a lovely wall hanging.

MATERIALS

Calico, percale, broadcloth, muslin are generally used for both the background and the appliqué pieces, but any closely-woven fabric that does not fray easily will do. Be sure that fabrics are preshrunk and colorfast. If washability is not a factor (as in a wall hanging), wools, velvets, and silks might be used. Fabrics of many textures will also add to the character of your work. Often a new sheet (plain white or in a color) is used as a background for a quilt.

For the stitchery, regular sewing thread in a color to match each individual appliqué piece is used. If the piece is being appliquéd with embroidery stitches, 6-strand floss or other embroidery threads are used.

EQUIPMENT

A regular sewing needle is used when the appliqué is blindstitched in place. A crewel needle is required if embroidery stitches are used. Appliqué is usually worked in the hand and a frame is not necessary.

METHOD

If your design (as for a quilt) requires many identical pieces, cut an actual-size pattern from cardboard for each element of the design. Place pattern on wrong side of fabric; pencil around. Repeat as many times as necessary, being sure to leave ½″ between pieces. If edges of pattern become worn with repeated use, replace with a new one. Repeat this process with each part of the design. Cut out pieces leaving ¼″ seam allowance all around (see illustration-Step 1). Separate pieces and place similar shapes in small plastic bags. They will remain clean and are easily identified in the transparent bags. **Note:** If only one or two pieces of a particular shape are needed, the design can be transferred directly to the fabric (see Index) without the use of a cardboard pattern.

Setting Pieces: Transfer entire pattern to background fabric. Prepare each appliqué piece by placing the cardboard pattern on wrong side of fabric, then press seam allowances over pattern (see illustration-Step 2). Clip seam allowances on curves and slash at corners to make them lie flat. It is wise to baste the seam allowance flat around all pieces. Place each piece right side up in its appropriate place on the background fabric. Baste in place.

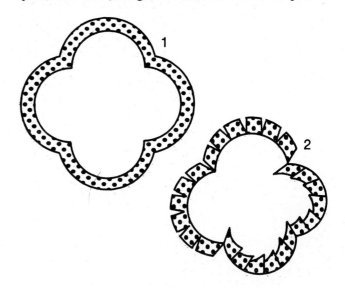

Two simple appliqué projects for beginners. Directions for tote bag and pillow are on page 68.

Appliquéing: Blind Technique: With sewing thread and sewing needle blind hem pieces in place. Slip stitch and overcast stitch can also be used for this method. The choice of stitch is not so important as the neatness and even length of the stitches. The edges of the appliqué pieces may then be decorated with a variety of embroidery stitches such as couching, feather stitch or chain stitch, but they are usually left plain. **Embroidery Technique:** After the appliqué pieces are basted in place, attach them permanently to the background fabric with embroidery stitches only. No sewing stitches are used in this technique. Buttonhole stitch is most commonly used (see Index). Work the stitches as closely together as necessary to hold the pieces neatly in place. Often the stitches can be so widely spaced that you are actually working a blanket stitch. Other stitches, such as satin or feather are also used to appliqué pieces in place. **Note:** The experienced needleworker may not bother pressing the seam allowance to the wrong side of the appliqué pieces. She will just turn in the edge and baste it. In this case it is helpful to mark the outline of the piece on the right side of the fabric at the very beginning.

TOTE BAG

With all the things that a woman finds it necessary to carry these days, a tote bag is almost as vital to her well being as a lipstick. This tote, in a particularly convenient size, was designed to introduce you to the basic technique of appliqué in the easiest manner possible. There are no difficult curved seams to turn and sew, no odd shapes to handle. On the other hand, the strict design of squares and stripes will lend itself to any number of color combinations. By the way, to keep the project simple we appliquéd just the front of the bag. You may want to gain extra experience in appliqué by decorating both the front and the back, however.

SIZE: 8¾"×14"×2½".

MATERIALS: 36"-wide firmly woven cotton, ½ yard each aqua and bright blue, small pieces of navy, cream and chartreuse; 36"-wide white nonwoven stiffening, ⅜ yard; sewing thread in colors to match fabrics; 2½"×8¾" piece stiff cardboard (optional).

EQUIPMENT: Sewing needle.

CUTTING: Bag (aqua): For front and back cut 2 pieces 9¾"×15". For side gussets cut 2 pieces 3½"×15". For bottom gusset cut 1 piece 3½"×9¾". For handles cut 2 pieces 2⅝"×11". **Lining** (bright blue): Cut pieces as for bag, omitting the 2 handle pieces. **Stiffening:** Cut pieces as for bag. **Appliqué Pieces:** Cut 2½" squares as follows: 2 cream, 2 bright blue, 4 navy. Cut 1¼"×9¾" strips as follows: 2 cream, 2 navy, 2 chartreuse, 1 bright blue.

APPLIQUÉ: Press ¼" seam allowances to wrong side on each edge of squares. On strips, on long edges only, press ¼" seam allowances to wrong side. Baste appliqué pieces to front of bag following photograph for color placement. Start with bottom strip ¾" above lower edge. Strips are ¼" apart. To position squares properly, work from center out to sides. Squares are 3/16" apart. When all pieces are basted, appliqué in place using the Blind Technique.

FINISHING: Baste stiffening to the wrong side of all bag pieces. Right sides together, pin and baste together all bag pieces (except handles) with ½" seams; stitch. Trim stiffening close to seams. Turn bag to right side. Assemble all lining pieces as for bag, making seams just a fraction wider than ½". Do not turn. On handles turn under ⅞" on each long edge. Turn under ¼" on long raw edge; slip stitch in place. Pin handles inside lining, raw ends at top edges and 1½" from side seams. Stitch across handles ½" from raw ends. Repeat stitching for extra strength.

Turn ½" at top edges of bag and lining to wrong side. Place lining in bag. Slip stitch together at top edge. If desired, place piece of stiff cardboard in the bottom of bag so that bag will retain its shape. For a neater appearance cardboard may be covered with fabric.

PILLOW

This chubby pillow with its bold confetti dots would make a cosy addition to a teenager's room or look just right tossed on an old-fashioned porch chair. You might consider this pillow as Step 2 in learning the various techniques of appliqué. You will learn how to handle curved edges on your appliqué pieces as well as how to appliqué with embroidery stitches. Even after mastering these skills you will probably want to make a second pillow. They are so pleasant to make, why stop with just one?

SIZE: 13" square.

MATERIALS: 36"-wide firmly-woven cotton, ⅜ yard pink, ½ yard red, small pieces of rose, orange and maroon; 6-strand embroidery floss in rose, orange and red; sewing thread in pink, red and white; ½ yard 36"-wide muslin (or good parts of an old sheet); 1 bag shredded foam rubber.

EQUIPMENT: Sewing needle; crewel needle.

CUTTING: For pillow form cut 2 pieces of muslin 14" square. For pillow cover cut 2 pieces of red cotton 14" square. For background of appliqué cut pink cotton 13" square. For appliqué pieces cut circles 4½" in diameter as follows: 1 red, 1 rose, 1 orange. Cut circles 3¼" in diameter as follows: 2 red, 3 orange, 4 rose. Cut 12 maroon circles 2¼" in diameter.

APPLIQUÉ: Enlarge diagram (each small square = 1" square) for pattern. Transfer pattern centering it on cotton square. On all circles press ¼" seam allowances to wrong side. Baste appliqué pieces in place on background following photograph for color arrangement. Circles should overlap (see broken lines on diagram). Join circles to background fabric with blanket stitch worked with 3 strands of floss in the same color as the circle being appliquéd. The only exceptions are the small maroon circles. Work these in rose floss in blanket stitches that are quite close together. **Note:** Work only those edges of circles that are exposed—not where they are overlapped.

FINISHING: For pillow form stitch the 2 muslin pieces together around edges with ½" seams, leaving 3" opening. Turn. Fill with foam rubber. Sew opening closed.

On pink square that has been appliquéd, press ½" seam allowances to wrong side. Center pink square on a red square; baste, then blind appliqué in place. Right sides together, stitch the 2 red squares together with ½" seams, leaving 10" open on 1 side. Turn and press. Slip in the pillow form. Turn in seam allowances on raw edges; slip stitch closed.

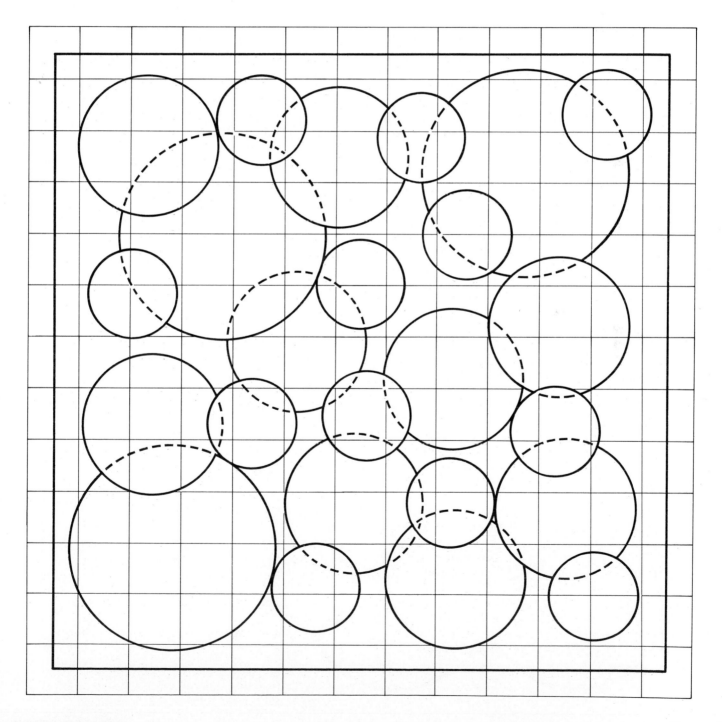

COVERLET

You don't have to be a grandmother to want to make a lavish layette for a new baby—but it helps. However, this gay young coverlet is so appealing that even a very young mother-to-be will want to try her hand at appliqué.

The design is similar to the little five-petal flowers of the print, although any pretty small-scale print is suitable. We feel that the bright colors are a new look for the very young, but you may prefer pastels for babies. In that case, choose the print first, then buy three suitable pastel cottons to combine with it.

SIZE: 25″×33″.

MATERIALS: 36″-wide cotton, 1¼ yards print, ¾ yard white, ⅜ yard each red, rose and orange; good section of an old blanket or ¾ yard blanketing or quilted fabric; sewing thread in red, rose, orange and background color of your print.

EQUIPMENT: Sewing needle.

CUTTING: Cut print backing 32″×40″. **Note:** The backing and print border for the front are in one piece. For background fabric for appliqué cut white cotton 25″×33″. For interlining cut blanket fabric 25″ x 33″. Trace the actual-size patterns below and make cardboard patterns for the flowers and flower center. Add ¼″ seam allowances on all the following pieces: Using large flower pattern cut 7 orange and 8 rose pieces. Cut 19 red pieces following small flower pattern. From print cut 15 centers.

APPLIQUÉ: Enlarge the diagram given on the "end papers" of this book (just inside the front or back cover), each small square = 1″ square. Transfer to white background fabric, centering design on fabric. On all appliqué pieces, press seam allowances to wrong side, clipping and slashing as necessary. Baste a center in place on each large flower. Appliqué by blind method. Baste large flowers in place on design following photograph for color arrangement. Blind appliqué to background. Blind appliqué all red flowers in place.

FINISHING: Put print backing face down on table. Center the blanket fabric on the backing. Pin and baste carefully from the center out. Stitch around edges of the interlining.

Place appliquéd section face up on interlining. Again working from center out, pin and baste carefully. Fold print edges to right side of carriage cover. Miter corners (for directions, see Index). Turn in ½″ on raw edges; blindstitch, taking care that your stitches do not go through to the back of the carriage cover. Also blindstitch down each miter at corners.

If desired, a few stitches can be worked right through the print centers of flowers to the back of cover to hold the interlining securely in place.

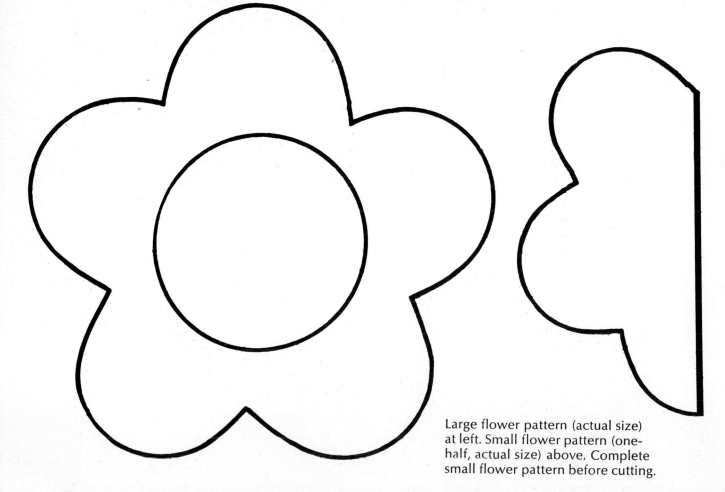

Large flower pattern (actual size) at left. Small flower pattern (one-half, actual size) above. Complete small flower pattern before cutting.

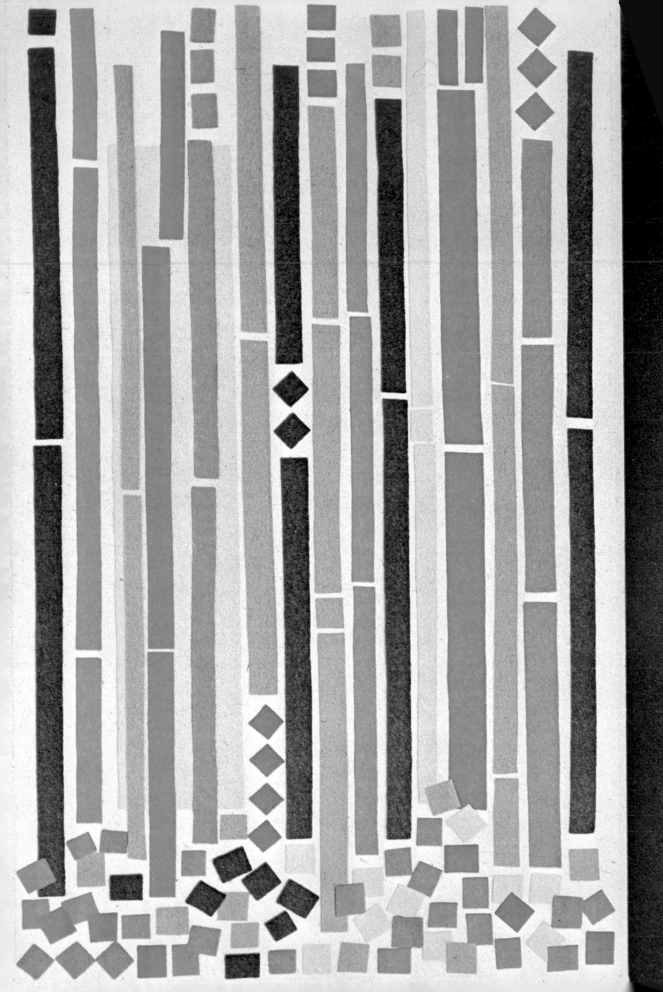

Pretend Appliqué

In this hectic age of superhighways, intercontinental jets, and trips to the moon, there is something incongruous about a needleworker spending endless hours on a single project (unless it is of heirloom quality). Although most of the designs in this book are not too time-consuming, we were particularly anxious to provide you with some activities which produce a great big effect without requiring too many of your precious minutes. Since the stitchery used in appliqué is what takes time, we've just eliminated thread and substituted glue instead. And that's why we've invented the new name — pretend appliqué.

Obviously this technique is suitable only for those items which will not get hard usage. Even if you are dedicated to delicate stitchery, do try the wall hanging or the picture! We think that you will enjoy the process so much that you may want to work out a picture frame, even a cover for a special book — or think of a dozen other uses for pretend appliqué.

MATERIALS

Any textured fabric — cotton, linen or wool — will make a suitable background. For the appliqué pieces, felt is the ideal material. It does not fray and therefore needs no turning in of the edges. Felt comes by the yard in 36″ or 72″ widths and is also available in 9″×12″ pieces, all in a wide range of colors. A number of glues are suitable. There is even a special fabric cement available. Ordinary liquid white glue (not paste) is recommended, however. A wonderful new iron-on bonding material also works well in this form of appliqué.

EQUIPMENT

A small brush is needed for use with glue; an iron and press cloth is needed to apply the bonding material. Use a soft pencil on felt.

METHOD

First transfer your prepared pattern to the background fabric. (Once you are experienced in this work it may be necessary to mark only a few key places on the background.) With a soft pencil, outline the appliqué pieces of felt; cut out. Working on one appliqué piece at a time, spread glue all over the back, making sure that you carry it right out to the edges. Place the piece in position on the background fabric and smooth it down, working from the center out. As each section of the design is completed, cover with a piece of paper, weight it down with a few books or magazines until the glue is dry.

Interesting new notions and needlework supplies are constantly being introduced. One that may be useful for your pretend appliqué is a bonding material which fuses fabric to fabric. It is available in sewing or notions departments. Cut out a piece large enough to fit your felt piece. With steam iron and press cloth fuse to the back of the felt, following directions that come with the bonding material. Remove backing. Your pattern pieces can be easily traced directly on this new material. Cut out pieces and fuse them to your background fabric, again following directions that come with the bonding material. **Note:** Touch up any loose felt pieces on overlaps, etc. with glue.

Simple felt strips play one subtle shade against another to produce this handsome contemporary picture. Even the novice needleworker can achieve professional results with this "pretend appliqué" technique.

PRETEND APPLIQUÉ PICTURE

This exciting contemporary picture is a particularly good example of the creative possibilities you will discover in pretend appliqué. Even if you develop it from the pattern given, you will find yourself shifting the pieces to satisfy your own esthetic sense.

SIZE: 12½"×20".
MATERIALS: ½ yard 36"-wide unbleached linen or natural-color textured cotton; 9"×12" felt pieces, 1 each of light olive, dark olive, grass green, emerald and jade; ⅛ yard 36"-wide chartreuse felt; white glue or 1 yard bonding material; 12½"×20" piece of firm but lightweight cardboard.
EQUIPMENT: Soft pencil; glue brush; iron and press cloth.
CUTTING: Enlarge diagram on page 76 (each small square = ½" square). Transfer pattern, centering it on a 16½"×24" piece of linen or cotton background fabric. This allows a 2" turn back all around. Following pattern, cut felt appliqué pieces in colors indicated by various shadings on diagram. **Note:** Cut a 2½"×13½" piece of chartreuse felt to go behind the 3rd, 4th and 5th main strips from the left on the diagram (see dotted lines). If you are using bonding material, follow preceding directions under Method, as well as directions that come with the material.

APPLIQUÉ: Join felt pieces to fabric background by gluing or bonding them in place. Overlap pieces where indicated by broken lines on diagram.
FINISHING: Press finished appliqué. Mount on cardboard (see Index for directions). Frame as desired.

BUTTERFLY WALL HANGING

A warm afternoon sun, golden field flowers, any number of bright vacation-time memories might be evoked by this wall hanging. Any butterfly expert would be hard pressed to give this gaudy creature its scientific name but we call it Midsummer. Do revive your memories of summers past—or build dreams of summers to come—by making a pretend butterfly in pretend appliqué.

SIZE: About 19"×23".
MATERIALS: ¾ yard 36"-wide unbleached linen or natural-color textured cotton; for lining ¾ yard 36"-wide orange cotton; 9"×12" felt pieces, 1 each of purple and orange, 2 of fuschia; white glue or ⅝ yard bonding material; sewing thread; 3 dressmaker's weights (optional).
EQUIPMENT: Soft pencil; glue brush; iron and press cloth.
CUTTING: Enlarge diagram for pattern, page 77 (each small square = 1" square). Complete other half of pattern reversing design. Cut linen or cotton background fabric 20"×24" and 1 long hanging strip 2½"×27". Cut orange cotton lining 20"×24". Baste vertical center line on the longer dimension of the background fabric, then transfer pattern to background fabric, centering it on center line and placing it so that lower point of butterfly comes 5" above lower edge of fabric. Following pattern for flower marked X on diagram, transfer 9 flowers across background fabric 1¼" above lower edge. Center first flower on center line and mark others ½" apart.

If you are using bonding material, follow preceding directions under Method, as well as directions that come with the material. Following pattern, cut 2 fuschia felt wings. From purple felt cut pieces for all shaded areas on diagram. Cut all other shapes from orange felt. Also cut 9 orange flowers following flower X on diagram. Cut 9 purple circles ½" in diameter.

APPLIQUÉ: Join felt wings to fabric background by gluing or bonding them in place, then join flowers and decorative trim to wings. Join little curved pieces around edges of wings. Adhere the flowers to lower edge of hanging, then add a purple circle to center of each.
FINISHING: Turn in ½" seam allowances on all edges of hanging and lining. Wrong sides together, slip stitch lining to hanging on sides and lower edge. Press hanging, turning in ½" seam allowances at top of hanging and lining. Fold hanging strip in half lengthwise. Stitch raw edges together with ¼" seam. Turn; press. From this piece cut 9 hanging tabs 3" long. Fold each in half crosswise. Insert ½" of raw ends of each in top of wall hanging, spacing them evenly across. Slip stitch hanging closed across top edge, catching in hanging tabs as you sew. If desired, sew weights to lining at lower corners and center of lower edge. See Index for general directions for wall hangings.

All outdoors is captured in this wall hanging composed of snippets of purple, orange and fuschia felt. Joined to the background by the "pretend appliqué" technique, it is easy enough for a youngster to do.

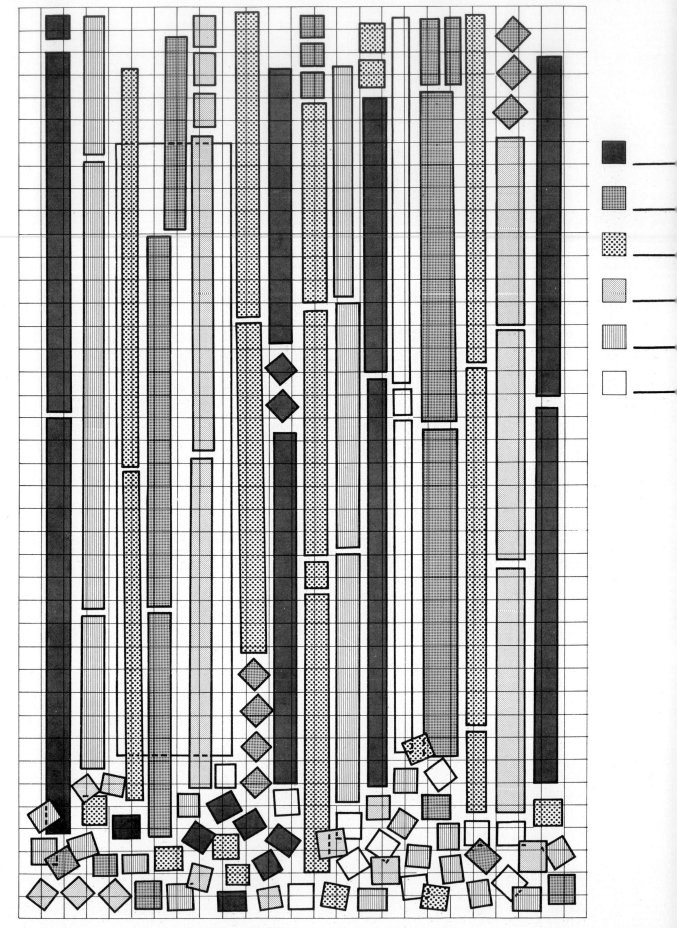

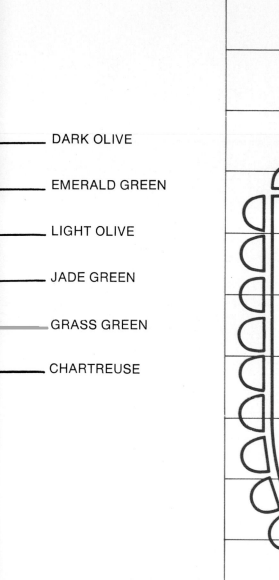

DARK OLIVE

EMERALD GREEN

LIGHT OLIVE

JADE GREEN

GRASS GREEN

CHARTREUSE

Pretend Appliqué Charts:
Contemporary Picture is
at left, Wall Hanging at
right. Directions, page 75.

Needlepoint

Visit any proud showplace of the American past and you will come across handsome examples of exquisite needlepoint worked by the great ladies who dwelt there. Mount Vernon treasures ten elegant chair cushions made by Martha Washington. Williamsburg is the home of any number of pieces of fine furniture upholstered in needlepoint lovingly worked over two centuries ago. How exciting to think that your needlework may be beautiful enough—and durable enough—to live down through the ages.

What is this special form of needlecraft that is marked by such elegance that it is as much at home in a palace as in a studio apartment? Very simply it is a form of embroidery in which stitches (usually worked in wool) completely cover the square meshes of canvas especially woven for the purpose. Often called tapestry, it took its name and often its designs—from the woven tapestries that graced the great baronial halls of Europe.

Traditionally, needlepoint was the handwork of ladies of wealth and leisure. The materials were expensive, the product unsuited to the rough log cabins of the American frontier. Fortunately that is no longer true. Excellent yarn and canvases are readily available. The designs and uses for needlepoint are as varied as the full range of contemporary taste. Since any department store carries needlepoint in traditional patterns, we have developed designs for you in a more modern idiom. They were also planned to give you experience in working different needlepoint stitches and, hopefully, to introduce you to a new leisure-time activity to be enjoyed for a lifetime.

TYPES OF NEEDLEPOINT

Since you are going to become an expert, it is wise to learn the proper terminology for the various forms of needlepoint. **Petit Point:** When the needlepoint is worked on canvas with 20 or more meshes to the inch, it is called petit point (little stitch). This delicate work is usually found on expensive imported evening bags or on the faces or other details of antique needlepoint pictures. **Needlepoint:** Beside being a general term, this word applies specifically to those pieces worked on canvas with 14

A rose is a rose . . . so much so that the vibrant needlepoint roses on this modern pillow top have even fooled the butterfly.

to 18 meshes to the inch. **Gros Point:** The average piece of needlepoint worked today is on canvas with 8 to 12 meshes per inch and is called gros point (big stitch). **Large Gros Point:** Handsome rugs— even wall hangings and cushions—can be worked on canvas with 3½ to 7 meshes per inch. For want of a better name it is called large gros point.

HOW TO BUY NEEDLEPOINT

Finished Design Details: Until recently most needlepoint pieces available in department stores had the design already worked. Only the background was left to be filled in. This may provide experience for the beginner but, hopefully, you will soon graduate to the more advanced—and more interesting— ways of working needlepoint. **Tramé Designs:** Sometimes you will find needlepoint pieces with the design indicated by long laid threads on the surface

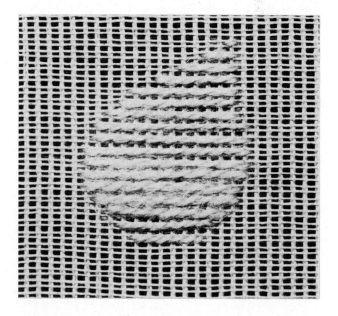

of the canvas (see photograph). These threads (called tramé threads) also indicate the color to be worked as well as the design. Half cross-stitch is always used on tramé pieces and is worked right over the tramé threads. This gives a slightly padded effect to the work. When the entire design is finished, the background is filled in in the usual manner. **Painted Designs:** It is now possible to find excellent needlepoint designs, both traditional and contemporary, painted directly on the canvas. These are easy to follow since your stitches are always worked in approximately the color indicated on the canvas. **Charted Designs:** Designs such as those on the following pages are worked out, stitch by stitch, on charts. The key accompanying each chart indicates the colors to be used. Each square on the chart indicates one stitch on the canvas.

MATERIALS

Canvas: Needlepoint is worked on canvas specially woven to produce evenly-spaced stitches of a given size. The size of the stitch depends on the number of meshes per inch of the canvas. Rug canvas may have as few as 3½ meshes per inch; petit point canvas as many as 40 meshes per inch. If a design calls for a particular size canvas, you may switch to another size. Remember, however, that the size of your finished piece of needlepoint will change. For example, if the design calls for canvas with 10 meshes to the inch and you use canvas with 14 meshes to the inch, your object will be smaller. Conversely, if you changed to canvas with 8 meshes to the inch, your finished piece will be larger.

Canvas comes in various widths, the most common being 27″ and 36″. Purchase the width that is the most economical for the work being planned. Canvas is available in single-thread and double-thread weaves (see photographs). Most needlepoint worked today is on double-thread canvas but delicate work (petit point) is always done on single-thread. Double-thread is usually ecru in color; single-thread is usually white.

Yarns: Although many smooth yarns may be used for needlepoint, so-called tapestry yarn is generally used. It is a firmly twisted yarn that does not fray easily, comes in handsome color ranges and in about 10 and 40 yard skeins. One or more strands of crewel embroidery wool is also frequently used for needlepoint. Occasionally one wants to introduce a shiny look to small areas of a design and embroidery thread in cotton, silk or synthetics may be added. **Note:** Dark backgrounds are often found on antique pieces and they make a fine contrast for modern designs. It is often more subtle, however, to use a very dark gray, a greenish black or a very dark blue rather than a true black on designs such as the rose pillow which follows.

In any case, the yarn must be the proper thickness to cover the canvas completely and yet not be so thick that it separates the threads of the canvas or frays when being worked. It is not easy to estimate the amount of yarn needed for a particular design but you can judge fairly well by working one square inch on your canvas in the yarn and stitch desired. Keep track of the amount used and multiply by the number of square inches of any given color in your design. Add an extra skein for loss by clipping ends, ripping, etc. Buy all the yarn (particularly for the background) at one time since later dye lots may differ slightly.

EQUIPMENT

Although most Americans work needlepoint in the hand (since the work can then be carried anywhere), it is highly recommended that you use a frame. It makes for much evener work and the canvas will remain in better shape and require less blocking when the piece is finished. The only other equipment necessary is a thimble, a scissors (since the yarn should be cut—never broken off) and a tapestry needle. This is a blunt needle with a large eye. They are generally found in sizes 18 to 22, the larger number being the finer needle. You may want to have a few since it is convenient to have one threaded with each color that is on your piece.

METHOD

Preparing Work: Always allow at least 2″ on all sides of the canvas beyond the area to be worked. To prevent fraying bind edges of canvas with masking tape or paint with white glue. If your canvas does not have the design already worked and you are not working from a chart, you may want to paint in the design. First trace the outline with waterproof ink on the canvas. Paint in each color area.

Although oil paints have always been used for this purpose, the new acrylic paints are particularly suitable. They are comparatively odor-free, dry rapidly and need only water for cleaning brushes.

If you are using a frame, turn back 1″ of canvas all around to form a double edge and lash to frame.

General Details: Use yarn cut not longer than 18″. Repeatedly pulling a longer length through the canvas will cause fraying and breaking. The design areas may be worked first and the background filled in later. If you are working from a chart, it will be easier to work the needlepoint row by row, however.

Begin a new yarn by making a knot. Leaving knot on right side, run yarn down through canvas about 1″ from where you want to begin. Bring needle up at starting point. After the stitches worked later cover the loose end of yarn, clip off the knot. When ending a length of yarn, run it back under a few stitches on wrong side of work.

BASIC STITCHES

Half Cross-stitch: The simplest of all needlepoint stitches is the half cross-stitch (see diagram). Always work from left to right. Start at the bottom of a stitch. Cross over 1 mesh of the canvas (diagonally) and insert needle for next stitch. Notice that the needle is always inserted in the vertical position. When the row of stitches is completed, turn work upside down so that next row can be worked from left to right.

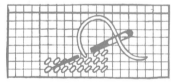

Tent Stitch: Petit point is always worked in this stitch. Since the work covers the back of the canvas as well as the front, it is also used for gros point when a particularly durable piece is required such as for chair seats, footstools or rugs. Remember that this stitch requires more yarn than the half cross-stitch. This stitch looks like the half cross-stitch on the surface but is worked from right to left. Bring needle out at bottom left corner of a

stitch. Cross over diagonally to upper right corner. Insert needle and cross behind stitch just completed to new stitch on left. When 1 row of stitches is completed, turn work upside down so that next row can also be worked from right to left.

Diagonal Stitch: This stitch is similar to tent stitch but is worked diagonally across the canvas. Note on the diagram that the needle is inserted horizontally. On the following row it will be inserted vertically. This stitch is used on backgrounds when a particularly even appearance is desirable.

Cross-Stitch: When a slightly more textured effect is desired, cross-stitch is often used for needlepoint. It is also used frequently with crosses 3½, 5 or 7 to 1″ for rugs. In working designs each cross-stitch is completed individually. On backgrounds, however, a row of half cross-stitch is completed, then the second half of the stitch is completed on the return (see diagram). In either case the stitches must all cross in the same direction.

Other Stitches: There are literally dozens of handsome stitches used in embroidery on canvas. A few that you may enjoy experimenting with are shown on page 89. Worked in rich colors, some are so decorative in themselves that they need no further pattern to produce a handsome effect.

BLOCKING

Frequently in doing needlepoint one pulls the canvas out of shape. Blocking will straighten out the work and will also make the stitches appear more even. If work is on a frame, it can be blocked right on the frame. If you have worked it in the hand, sponge **the wrong side** of the needlepoint until yarn and canvas are wet but not saturated. Stretch piece into proper shape and fasten to a board with rust-proof tacks placing them not more than 1″ apart. Let dry thoroughly. If work is still out of shape, repeat the process.

NEEDLEPOINT PILLOW

Roses and needlepoint are as closely related in our minds as hearts and Valentine's Day. On this chic modern pillow, however, an exotic new breed of roses unknown to any horticultural society makes its first appearance. Worked in vibrant shades of orange, magenta, scarlet and hot pink, these full-blown beauties are scattered on an inky black background to produce marvelous color impact.

The color areas were deliberately kept bold and sharp so that the chart can be followed easily by the beginner. A simple half cross-stitch is used throughout.

SIZE: About 11″×14″.

MATERIALS: ½ yard 27″ double-mesh needlepoint canvas, 10 meshes to 1″; 30-yard cards of crewel yarn, 1 orange, 1 magenta, 1 scarlet, 2 hot pink, 6 bright green and 7 black; masking tape; 12″×15″ piece of firm black cotton or wool for pillow back; 2 pieces of muslin 12″×15″ for inner pillow; sewing thread; 1 bag shredded foam rubber.

EQUIPMENT: Embroidery frame; tapestry needle.

PREPARING CANVAS: Cut canvas 15″×18″. Bind edges, turn them under and place piece in frame following general directions given at the beginning of this section.

NEEDLEPOINT: Use 3 strands of crewel wool throughout. Using half cross-stitch, work directly from chart. Each square on the chart indicates 1 stitch in the color specified by the key. Once you have the "feel" of working needlepoint, you may want to work an entire area of a single color (such as a leaf) rather than complete a row at a time.

FINISHING: Block piece. Cut off excess canvas, leaving ½″ all around. Turn this under and baste around edges. For inner pillow stitch the 2 muslin pieces together around edges with ½″ seam allowances, leaving a 3″ opening. Turn and stuff with shredded foam rubber. Sew opening closed. Turn under and press ½″ seam allowances all around piece of black cotton or wool. With wrong sides together whip (with small stitches) this piece to needlepoint piece, leaving an 8″ opening on 1 end. Slip in inner pillow and whip opening closed.

NEEDLEPOINT PICTURE

A make-believe ship sails a make-believe sea on this imaginative picture. Even a make-believe wind blows East and West at the same time! Or how could those little flags be carrying on the way they do?

The variety of rich colors and the amusing design make this picture a delight to work and a pleasure to own. The simple square shape can easily be converted to a pillow as well. Although the stitch used is the basic half cross-stitch, the frequent color changes will give the less-experienced needleworker valuable practice.

SIZE: About 12″ square.

MATERIALS: ½ yard single-mesh needlepoint canvas, 12 meshes to 1″; 30-yard cards crewel yarn, 5 blue gray, 5 medium aqua, 3 marine blue, 1 peacock blue, 1 bright orange, 1 burnt orange, 1 magenta, 1 gray violet; masking tape; piece of firm but lightweight cardboard.

EQUIPMENT: Embroidery frame; tapestry needle.

PREPARING CANVAS: Cut canvas 16″ square. Bind edges, turn under and place piece in frame following general directions given at the beginning of this section.

NEEDLEPOINT: Use 3 strands of crewel wool throughout. Using half cross-stitch and working a stitch in each mesh of canvas, work directly from chart. Each square on chart indicates 1 stitch in the color specified by the key. Note: To make the chart easier to follow we omitted the color changes on the background. The background alternates rows of blue gray and medium aqua. Work bottom row of picture in blue gray; work next row in medium aqua. Alternate these 2 rows all the way to the top row which is blue gray. The center 9 stitches of each flower are also blue gray.

FINISHING: Block piece. Cut cardboard the exact size of your needlepoint area. Attach needlepoint to cardboard (see Index for directions). Frame as desired.

Needlepoint designs don't have to be serious! This happy little ship sailing in a sea of flowers is an example of the modern approach to needlework design. This picture would add a bright note to any room.

⊞ GREEN	⊠ MAGENTA	
▨ HOT PINK	⊞ SCARLET	
⊡ ORANGE	⊟ BLACK	

 MARINE BLUE

 PEACOCK BLUE

 BRIGHT ORANGE

BURNT ORANGE

 MAGENTA

GRAY-VIOLET

NEEDLEPOINT DESK SET

There are many times you will want to create a gift that is not too personal but that shows you cared enough to spend time and effort on it. Perhaps you are a patient who wants to express her gratitude to her doctor beyond the prompt payment of a bill. Or you may want to produce a gift that is just right to present to a husband and a wife or even an entire family. For this reason we have come up with this design for a desk set that would look great on a teak desk in a modern family room yet is elegant enough for a traditional desk in a more formal living room. The needlepoint pieces work up quickly and will also give you experience in working cross-stitch on canvas.

SIZE: Blotter strips, about 1⅞″×12¼″; pencil cup, about 4″ high × 3¼″ in diameter; telephone book, about 4⅜ ×6⅜″.

MATERIALS: For 3-piece desk set: ½ yard 36″ single-mesh needlepoint canvas, 14 meshes to 1″; 10-yard skeins tapestry yarn, 7 black, 5 camel, 3 off-white; masking tape; pencil cup 4″ high × 3¼″ in diameter; ½ yard 36″ firmly-woven black cotton; 12¼″×19″ piece of firm cardboard; desk blotter; looseleaf telephone book 4⅜″×6⅜″; black sewing thread.

EQUIPMENT: Tapestry needle; sewing needle.

PREPARING CANVAS: Mark the 2 blotter strips 1⅛″×12¼″ on canvas so that they are at least 2″ apart and 2″ from edges of canvas. Cut out this area. Mark area for pencil cup 4″×10″ and for telephone book 6⅜″×10″ on remaining canvas, leaving 2″ spaces as before. Bind edges of both pieces of canvas following general directions given at the beginning of this section. Since the needlepoint areas are small, it is not necessary to use a frame.

NEEDLEPOINT: Use cross-stitch throughout and work each stitch over **2** horizontal and **2** vertical threads of the canvas. Work directly from the charts. Each square on charts indicates 1 stitch in the color specified.

Blotter Strips: For each strip follow chart working from bottom row up to the top. Omitting the row marked Center, repeat chart from top down to bottom row.

Pencil Cup: Work entire chart. However, if your basic cup differs in size from the given measurements, adjust the design accordingly. If your cup is higher, add a black border to top and bottom edges; if cup is lower, omit a row or two on top and bottom edges. If diameter of cup is larger, add rows at sides of strip; if smaller, omit a row or two at sides.

Telephone Book: Follow chart from A to B then continue on for back cover of book by omitting center row of stitches and repeat chart back to A. If your book differs slightly in size, add (or subtract) a row or two of border stitches.

FINISHING: Block pieces.

Blotter: Cut out blotter strips leaving ½″ of canvas all around each. Fold allowances to wrong side and sew invisibly in place. Cut black cotton 13¼″ ×20″. Hem long edges so that width of piece is exact size of needlepoint strips. Turn in ½″ at 1 end of cotton piece. Lay needlepoint strip over end and whip in place around the 3 outer edges, leaving inner edge of strip free. Repeat at other end. Slip cardboard under blotter strips. A regular desk blotter may then be cut to fit the cardboard and slipped in place.

Pencil Cup: Cut out needlepoint piece leaving ½″ allowances all around. Fold allowances on each short end to wrong side and fasten down with masking tape. Bring the 2 short ends of piece together and join with whip stitch. Fold remaining 2 seam allowances to wrong side and fasten with masking tape. Slip needlepoint over pencil cup.

Telephone Book: Cut out needlepoint piece leaving ½″ allowances all around. Fold allowances to wrong side and sew invisibly in place. Cut 2 pieces black cotton 5¼″×7½″ (or to fit 1 side of your needlepoint cover—not including the spine—and adding ½″ all around). Turn ½″ allowances to wrong side all around each piece. Wrong sides together, pin a cotton piece to 1 side of needlepoint cover, starting at side edge and reaching as far as spine. Whip cotton to needlepoint around outside edges. Hem black cotton along edge that meets spine but do not fasten down. Repeat with the cotton piece of other side of cover. Cut 2 black cotton pieces 1¾″ square. Fold about ¼″ to wrong side all around. Pieces should be exact width of spine. Sew a piece in place at top and bottom of inside of spine to cover bare canvas. Slip telephone book into needlepoint cover.

Any writing penned on this elegant desk blotter is sure to have literary merit—even if it's only a grocery list. Directions are for blotter, pencil cup and telephone book. See page 88 for the charts.

CENTER ➤

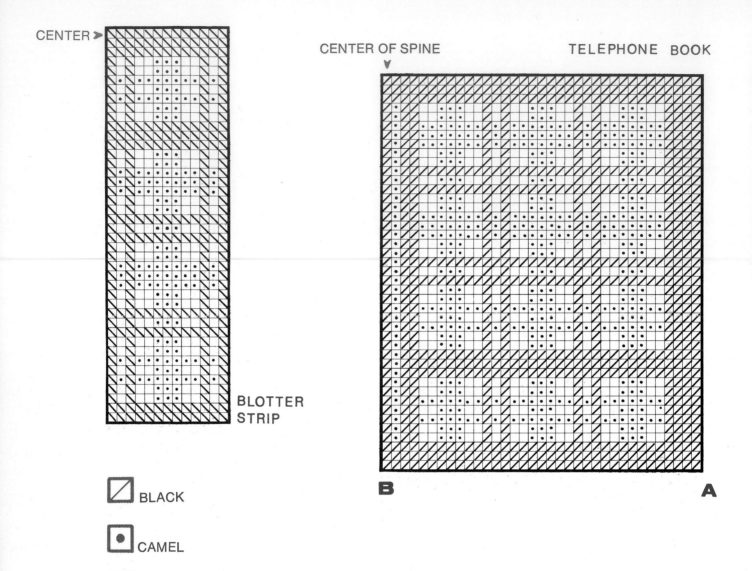

BLOTTER STRIP

☑ BLACK

▣ CAMEL

☐ OFF WHITE

B

A

PENCIL CUP

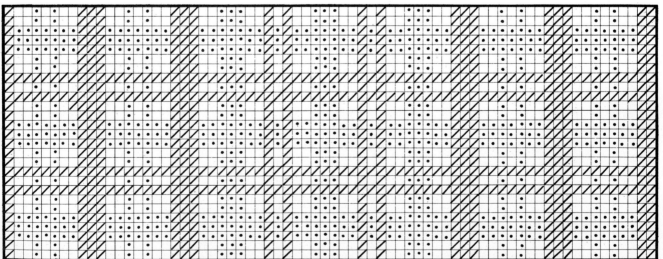

ADDITIONAL NEEDLEPOINT STITCHES

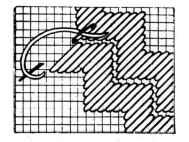

Byzantine Stitch: This stitch is used to cover large areas quickly. It gives the effect of a woven fabric. Work satin stitches diagonally over 4 vertical and 4 horizontal threads and form steps as shown.

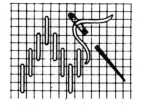

Florentine Stitch: This stitch forms zigzag patterns known as Florentine work. Work straight stitches over 4 threads of canvas, making each stitch 2 threads above (or below) the last one. This stitch is particularly attractive when worked in 3 or 4 shades of 1 color, each row across being worked in just 1 shade.

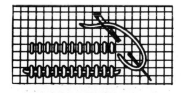

Hungarian Stitch: This is a variation of the Florentine Stitch, also called Bargello Work, also called Flame Stitch. The terms are used interchangeably. Make groups of 3 upright stitches, working over 2, 4 then 2 horizontal threads of canvas. Alternate rows so all spaces are filled. This stitch may be worked in 1 color or in 2 as shown.

Checker Stitch: There are a number of variations of Checker (sometimes called Checkerboard) Stitch. This is just one for you to experiment with. It can be worked in 1 or 2 colors. Make a square of 16 small half cross-stitches as shown. Alternate with a square of 7 stitches graduated in size. Follow diagram for number of threads to work over.

Gobelin Stitch, Encroaching: This stitch is often used for shading or to cover large areas quickly. Work stitches over 5 horizontal threads and slant diagonally over 1. The next row overlaps the last by 1 thread of canvas.

Jacquard Stitch: Make rows in steps, working 1 row over 2 vertical and 2 horizontal threads of canvas and the next row half cross-stitches over 1 intersection.

Cross-stitch, Double: This stitch works up faster than the usual small cross-stitch. Make a cross-stitch over the number of threads shown, then work another cross-stitch diagonally over it.

Gobelin Stitch, Upright: This stitch is usually worked on single-mesh canvas. Work stitches over 2 horizontal threads as shown at top of diagram. Sometimes a thread is laid across the canvas first and the stitches are worked over it as shown in lower part of diagram.

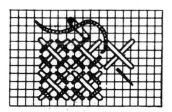

Rice Stitch: First cover background with large cross-stitches worked over 4 vertical and 4 horizontal threads of canvas. Over corners of each cross-stitch make small diagonal stitches at right angles to each other. Cross-stitches are often worked in a heavier weight yarn.

PATRIOTIC HANDBAG

Makes you think of George M. Cohan, the Fourth of July and all those grand old things, doesn't it? It's amazing just what the colors red, white and blue can do to a design. This handbag is in the same basic pattern as the desk set yet in this combination of colors the design takes on an entirely new look.

Even though you may have made the desk set, don't hesitate working the design again. This time around you will learn a brand-new needlepoint stitch and will also learn how to combine two stitches in one design.

SIZE: About 8½"×10½".

MATERIALS: ⅜ yard 27" single-mesh needlepoint canvas, 12 meshes to 1"; 10-yard skeins tapestry yarn, 4 red, 2 white and 6 blue; masking tape; piece of blue textured wool or cotton for back of bag and handles; blue silk for lining; small amount dressmaker's non-woven interfacing; 9½" zipper; blue sewing thread.

EQUIPMENT: Tapestry needle; sewing needle.

PREPARING CANVAS: Cut canvas 12½"×14½". Bind edges following directions given at beginning of this section. It is not necessary to use a frame.

NEEDLEPOINT: Follow chart for color placement. Each square on the chart indicates 1 stitch in the color specified by the key. First work all the blue, then all the red sections in twist stitch (see diagram). Lastly work all white areas in cross-stitch.

FINISHING: Block piece. Trim canvas so there are ½" seam allowances all around. Cut interfacing 8½"×10½"; center on back of needlepoint and tack with a few stitches. Turn under seam allowances of canvas and baste.

Back of Bag: Cut 1 piece of wool or cotton 8"× 11½" and 1 piece 2½"×11½". Cut interfacing 7"× 10½" and 1½"×10½". Center interfacing pieces on similar wool or cotton pieces (interfacing pieces have no seam allowances); baste. Join long edges of the 2 pieces, stitching only at each end, leaving center 9½" open for zipper. Insert zipper. (**Note:** Zipper is near top of bag.) Turn under seam allowances on all outer edges; baste.

Handles: Cut 1 piece of wool or cotton 1½"×11". Fold in thirds lengthwise; turn in raw edge ¼". Slip stitch closed. Tack ends of handle to wrong side of needlepoint piece 2½" from each side edge. Make another handle and tack to back of bag in same manner.

Lining: Cut lining pieces 9½"×11½", 8"×11½" and 2½"×11½". Turn in ½" seam allowances on edges of all pieces. Slip stitch to back of corresponding parts of bag. **Note:** It may be necessary to turn in a fraction of an inch more along zipper edges.

Wrong sides together, pin back of bag to needlepoint piece carefully and whip together around all sides.

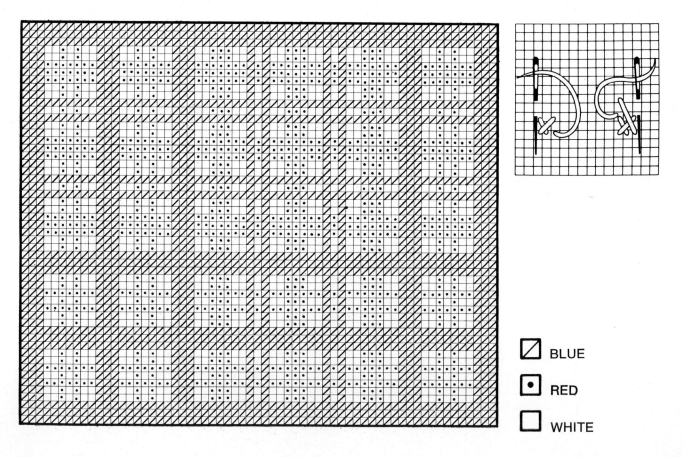

☑ BLUE

⊡ RED

☐ WHITE

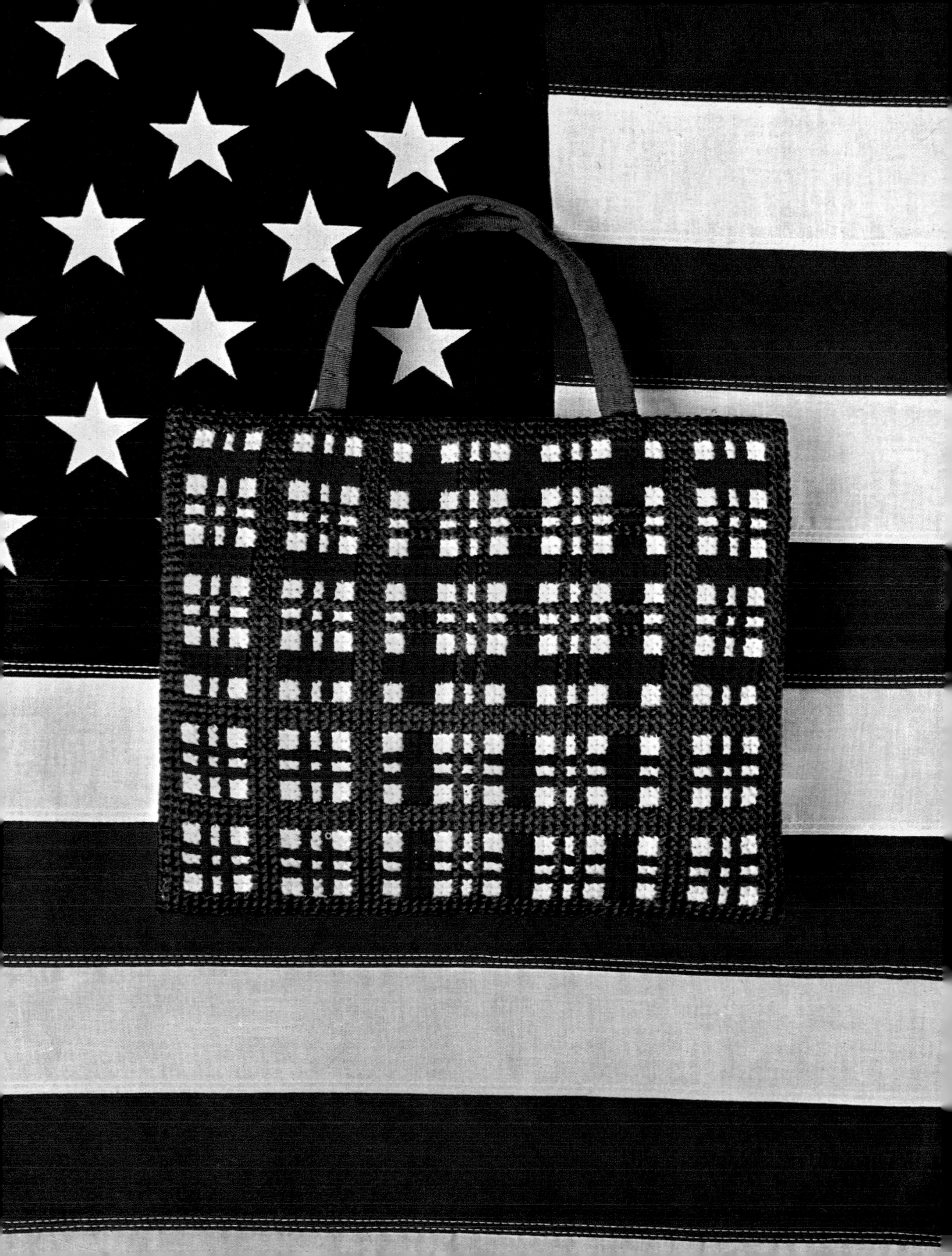

ABSTRACT DESIGN IN LARGE GROS POINT

Now that you are an expert you may want to try your hand at needlepoint where you can exercise your creativity. Here's a bold design in large gros point for you to play with. Perhaps you would enjoy working it in other colors. The photograph shows a sketch of an alternate color concept.

You could make the piece just as it is for a pillow top. Or you could extend the design, work it on even larger mesh canvas and come up with a breathtaking hall runner. Worked on a finer mesh canvas, the design might make a smashing modern handbag. Give your imagination free rein!

SIZE: About 14″ square.

MATERIALS: ½ yard double-mesh needlepoint canvas, 5 meshes to 1″; 1-oz. skein wool rug yarn, 1 each brick red, purple, deep rose, pink; masking tape.

EQUIPMENT: Large tapestry or rug needle.

PREPARING CANVAS: Cut canvas 18″ square. Bind edges; turn them under and place piece in frame following general directions given at beginning of this section.

NEEDLEPOINT: Use 1 strand of rug yarn throughout. Using half cross-stitch, work directly from chart. Each square on the chart indicates 1 stitch in the color specified by the key.

FINISHING: Block piece. Finish as desired.

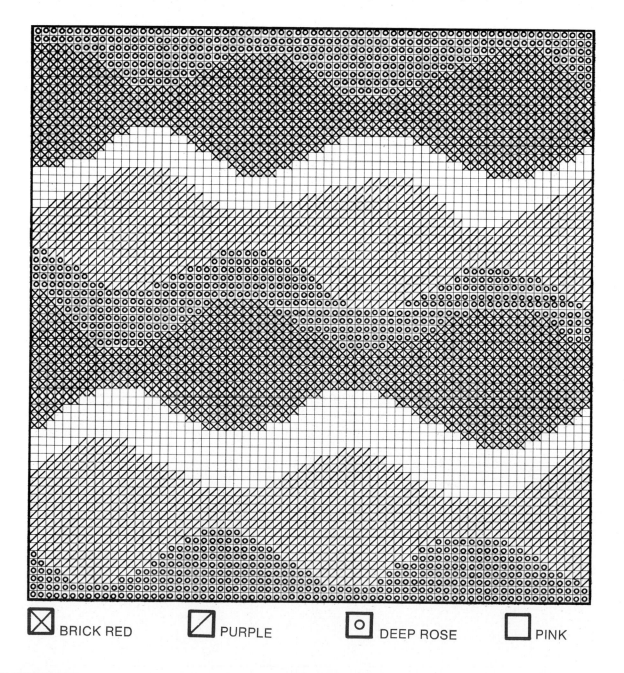

⊠ BRICK RED   ⧄ PURPLE   ⊙ DEEP ROSE   ☐ PINK

Rug Making

When we talk of primitive peoples, we sometimes classify them by the kind of floor they had. We even speak of a certain historic figure of more recent times as having come from a "dirt-floored cabin." Actually the earliest furnishings were probably a pile of leaves or perhaps animal skins, which served as bed and sitting area. It's hard to imagine that these "rugs" were the forebears of our rugs today!

Perhaps it's human nature to want to protect ourselves from the cold and hardness of our floors, whether they are made of packed earth, parquet or marble. For many centuries, people used whatever large fur or textile items they had as floor coverings. Old tapestries came down from the walls to serve as rugs. In the cold north countries of Europe, the heavy bed covers moved down to the floors.

We have access to such handsome and practical floor coverings today that we had better have some pretty strong motivation to put our efforts into producing a rug. In case you need some reasons to bolster your resolve to make a rug, here are a few that we believe are valid.

1. A rug, if you plan it carefully, may cost almost nothing to make—and saving money is one of the best reasons for rug making that we can think of. Yarn raveled from old sweaters, woolen strips cut from garments gathered from friends, mill ends—all may be the basic material of an exquisite rug. The writer of this book worked in a large institution many years ago where the floors were covered with hundreds of beautiful Oriental-type rugs hooked and woven by the patients from the ravelings of old burlap potato sacks!

2. There are fashions in rugs as there are in everything else. When low pile rugs are in style, just try to find a high pile one! If almond green is the current color and you have your heart set on a rug with a gray background, you can cover every store in town and never find the one you really want. Make your own rug and you can have the exact color, size, type and design that you know is perfect for your home.

3. If the two preceding reasons for making a rug have not already put you to work, let's talk about satisfaction. Perhaps there is no more gratifying experience than surveying a job well done. Just think how great you would feel if the rug that greets your guests at the front door was a product of your own hands. Unlike many items of needlework, a rug is never put away. It is always there to attest to your skill, persistence and artistry! Need we say more?

TYPES OF RUGS

There are almost as many ways to make a rug as there are forms of needlework. Although giving directions for all of them is beyond the scope of this book, let us mention a few. Knitting and crocheting are excellent ways of producing rugs with a "country" look. They work up fast and are especially good in kitchens or family rooms where washability is a factor.

Braided rugs are known to all of us. Even if the colonial style of decorating (where they are used most often) is not yours, a braided rug can find a place in almost any home.

Woven rugs may be as simple as the old-time "rag rug" or as elaborate as the most exquisite tapestry. We sincerely hope that a few of our readers will "graduate" to this exciting craft.

Rugs can also be embroidered. Occasionally examples are found in which the entire rug consists of basic embroidery stitches worked in heavy wools on burlap. More often one sees lovely cross-stitch rugs worked in wool on burlap or on rug canvas. Rugs can also be worked in many of the other needlepoint stitches. In fact, some of the designs in the needlepoint section (the pillow, the purse or the abstract design, for example) would make handsome rugs worked on a large scale.

Although the preceding methods of making rugs (and many other methods) are fascinating, we shall concentrate on the rya rug, the traditional hooked rug and the latch hooked rug. General information about the techniques and directions for making a rug by each method follow.

RYA RUGS

In Scandinavia, the early peoples slept on and under animal skins to find a measure of warmth in the endless, bitterly cold winter nights. The skins were always used with the fur side in. It may not have been very sanitary but it must have been cozy. Generations later when skills had been developed and sheep had been domesticated, the people of these Northern lands began to make their bed covers—and quite naturally they made them as much like animal skins as possible. The smooth surface was used on top, the warm pile on the bottom of their rya. These primitive covers were woven on a loom.

The cool blue of Northern lakes, the rough bark of tall pines and the pale gold light of a winter sun have been the inspiration for this rug made by the rya method. Directions for it are on pages 97 and 98.

Much later, as further skills developed, the Scandinavian bed began to be dressed with hand-woven linen sheets and hand-woven wool blankets. But the thrifty peasant was not about to discard his beloved rya. He just turned it over and, pile side up, began using it for a day-time coverlet. It was not too long before it occurred to some smart Scandinavian that a rya would be ideal to keep the cold winds from whistling up through the floor boards.

MATERIALS

To discuss materials for these rugs it is necessary to talk a little about techniques. The original rya was woven on a loom, the basic thread being wool or linen. The pile which was knotted in during the weaving was most often wool but could also be linen, cut-up rags or a combination of all three. Later a new technique (see Method) was developed in which the pile was sewn to a fabric background. This fabric is a sturdy linen especially woven for the purpose. Since it is difficult to find (and expensive) in the United States, we just substituted rug burlap which is available in many needlework departments.

The pile in the early rya was made of wool plucked directly from the sheep so the colors were usually just the natural color of wool with an occasional cross or simple design worked in the wool from (can you believe it?) a black sheep! Later on the wool (linen and rags, too) were dyed. Although modern ryas can be very colorful, the most traditional ones use the muted colors obtained when wools were dyed with natural materials such as berries or bark. To get this effect it is suggested that you use yarn of worsted weight in what the manufacturers call heather tones.

EQUIPMENT

The only special item you need is a rug needle with a large eye. No frame is used.

METHOD

Cut burlap to size of rug desired, allowing for 2" to 4" margins all around. If you can leave selvages for the time being, so much the better. Whip raw edges to prevent fraying.

Thread 1 or 2 strands of yarn cut 25" to 1 yard long and practice the rya knot on scrap burlap (see diagrams). Work row of knots from left to right as follows: Leaving 2" end of yarn on right side of fabric, take needle from right to left behind 2 threads of burlap. Insert needle behind 2 new threads of burlap and pull up yarn (rya knot formed). You will note that the knot goes over 4 threads of burlap. Make stitch behind 2 new threads of burlap but pull up yarn only far enough to leave loop of desired length. Diagram shows how each new knot anchors a loop in place. Make these loops desired length by using 2 or 3 fingers of left hand as a gauge or cut a cardboard gauge 5" long by desired width.

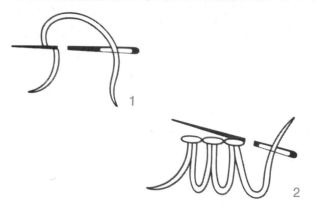

When a row of knots has been completed, cut off yarn, leaving end on right side of work as at beginning. Now cut loops to form pile. Each row of knots is worked above the preceding row. Leave 6 horizontal threads of burlap between rows. When entire rug is finished, clip the pile again to even it up as necessary.

FINISHING

Cut off margins, leaving 2" all around. Turn under raw edges and hem or line entire rug. Read directions under Finishing Hooked Rugs for further suggestions.

RYA RUG

This handsome little rug has many of the basic characteristics of the traditional rya. The colors are soft and muted. The design is simple and geometric. And it does make you want to dig your toes into the luxurious warm pile! Make it following the chart on page 98.

SIZE: About 32"×38".
MATERIALS: 39"-40" rug burlap, 1¼ yards; knitting worsted in heather tones, 10 ozs. medium blue, 10 ozs. oxford gray, 12 ozs. golden brown, 24 ozs. dark brown.
EQUIPMENT: 3 large-eyed rug needles.
PREPARING BURLAP: Leave selvages on side edges. Cut burlap 42" long. Whip raw ends. Centering it, mark an area 32"×38" on burlap.

Here's a small section of a latch hook rug that can be developed to fit most size rooms. See page 100.

◉ GOLDEN BROWN **⊠ DARK BROWN** **◻ BLUE AND GRAY**

KNOTTING RUG: Thread 1 needle with 4 strands of dark brown yarn, 1 needle with 4 strands of golden brown and 1 needle with 2 strands of blue and 2 strands of gray. Narrow end toward you, place burlap on a table. Start at this end with dark brown. Inside left edge of marked area begin first row of knots (bottom row of chart). Each symbol on chart indicates 1 knot in the color indicated by the key. Gauge length of loops by working over 3 fingers. Work 1 complete row before going on to the next. **Note:** On the chart there is a row of empty squares between each row of symbols. This indicates 6 horizontal threads of burlap skipped between rows of knots. Continue to top of chart; omit row marked Center and follow chart back to bottom.

FINISHING: Follow general directions for finishing rya rugs at beginning of this section as well as general suggestions for Finishing Hooked Rugs.

LATCH HOOK RUGS

For centuries, the most beautiful rugs in the world have been made in the Middle East and the Orient. Unfortunately those areas, too, have succumbed to industrialization. Only a few rugs are still made by hand with the Oriental knot that is the basic method of producing them. On the other hand, we who have been released from drudgery by just such industrilization now have the leisure to pick up where the Persians left off.

The knot produced by a latch hook is very similar to the knot used in Oriental rugs. Although a few ardent needleworkers made knotted rugs down through the years, it is only in the last few years that latch hook rugs have become popular and are even outstripping the traditional hooked rug in popularity in parts of the United States.

The technique is easy and the results are ensured since the evenness of the pile and regularity of the knots is not dependent on skill. Each knot is made of a measured length of yarn pulled through an open-meshed canvas. You will learn to make the knot in a minute and can have a rug under way in no time.

MATERIALS

The backing is always a heavy double-thread rug canvas (sometimes called Smyrna canvas). It comes 28" or 30", 36" and 40" wide. Buy the most economical width for the rug you are planning. The canvas may have 3½, 4 or 5 meshes to 1". The filling is usually wool rug yarn which you may buy by the ounce and cut as needed. However, convenient ready-cut lengths of rug yarn may be purchased in bundles of one color to use in this type of rug.

EQUIPMENT

No frame is needed for latch hooked rugs. You will need a latch hook (sometimes called a latchet hook). If you are not using ready-cut yarn, you may find a commercial yarn cutter handy, although it is not a necessity. A rug needle may be needed to hem and bind the rug.

METHOD

Preparing Canvas: Many latch hook rug kits are readily available by mail order or in needlework departments. To work out your own rug design make a full-size pattern. Lay the canvas over it, allowing sufficient canvas outside pattern for hems. With a felt-tipped pen draw the outlines of the pattern which will show through the meshes of the canvas. If you want to indicate colors to follow, paint them with acrylic paints as described in the Needlepoint section or rough them in with crayon. **Note:** Since each knot is a separate entity, patterns can also be worked out from charts as is the rug which follows these general directions.

To prevent the raw ends of canvas from fraying, bind with masking tape. Keep selvages on canvas until rug is finished.

Knotting: If you are not using ready-cut yarn, prepare at least 50 pieces of each color needed by cutting 2½" lengths (or use a yarn cutter).

Place canvas on table with narrow end toward you. Start at the right edge of marked area and work first knot as follows: Fold piece of yarn in half over shank of hook (Diagram 1). Insert hook into first hole, go under double horizontal threads and come up through hole directly above (Diagram 2). Draw hook back, catching the 2 loose ends of yarn (Diagram 3). Let go of ends of yarn and draw hook toward you until loose ends have been pulled through looped yarn. Tighten knot by pulling ends firmly (Diagram 4). Continue knots across row. Work each row from right to left. Roll up completed work in your lap.

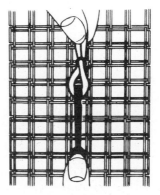
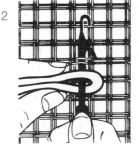
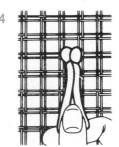

FINISHING

Brush rug to remove fuzz and lint. Clip off uneven ends of yarn. Cut off any extra canvas, leaving 1″ hem allowances. Fold to wrong side; baste. Cover with rug binding sewn around edges. Rug may also be lined or treated with non-skid liquid as described under Finishing Hooked Rugs.

Note: Hem allowances may be folded to front of rug and basted in place *before* any knotting is done. The knots are then worked through the double thickness as the rug is made.

GEOMETRIC RUG

Bold colors and a bold design join in this horizontally striped latch hook rug that could easily be the most decorative feature of any room. The design was carefully developed so that you can extend the size of the rug to fit any of your decorating needs. If you would like to make a hall runner, great! Just make it the width you need and keep adding stripes until the runner is as long as required. In fact, this versatile rug will fit in almost anywhere—unless you have an octagonal room!

SIZE: As desired.
MATERIALS: Double-thread canvas, 4 meshes to 1″ (amount depends on size rug desired); 1-oz. bundles ready-cut wool rug yarn, 1½ orange, 1½ medium blue, ½ skipper blue, 1 dark brown (amounts indicate a generous quantity for an area worked the size of chart); masking tape; rug binding; heavy thread.
EQUIPMENT: Latch hook; rug needle.
PREPARING CANVAS: Plan size of rug carefully. Area shown on chart is about 5½″×13¼″. Cut canvas allowing 2″ all around for hems. Leave selvages if possible. Bind all raw edges with masking tape.
KNOTTING: Follow chart for design. Each symbol on chart indicates 1 knot in the color specified. Start at right side and bottom row of chart and work each row across, repeating as many times as necessary for the width of your rug. When you reach the top of chart, repeat stripes as necessary for the length of your rug. For example, a small rug might have a *total* of stripes A - B - C - D - C - E - C - D - C - E - C - D - C - B - A.
FINISHING: Cut off selvages and trim hem allowances to 1″. Finish with rug binding or in any way given in the general directions.

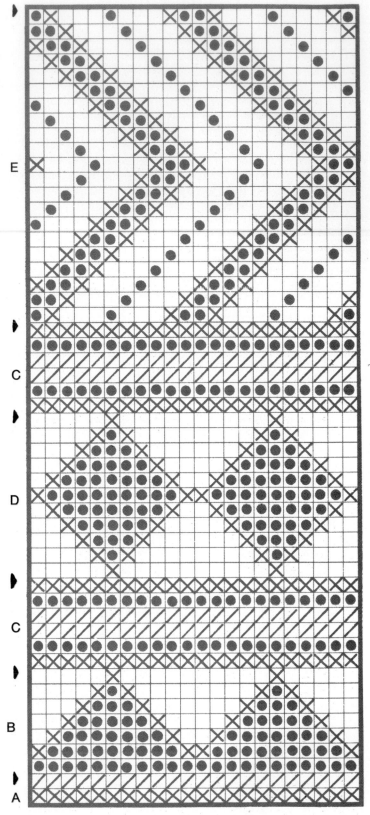

 SKIPPER BLUE   DARK BROWN   ORANGE   MEDIUM BLUE

HOOKED RUGS

Hooking is quite simply the technique of drawing little loops of yarn or strips of fabric through the weave of a heavy backing fabric. Although it was done for centuries in many parts of the world, the technique was not used for rug making until thrifty housewives in Colonial America began hooking their treasured scraps into hand-woven backing fabric and creating rugs. Only a few of these can be found in museums that specialize in Americana but they attest to the skill and patience of our forebears.

The designs of the rugs were as varied as the lives of the women who made them. Flowers in garlands, bouquets and borders were a favorite motif, of course. However some of the most appealing rugs were more personal and depicted elements in the maker's daily life. Often a favorite pet—a dog, a horse, a kitten—was memorialized on a rug. The farmhouse itself—or even the barn—served as inspiration for a rug design. But don't think that all our ancestors were so creative! Actually the ladies of the Colonies traded their rug patterns just as we trade recipes. And about 100 years ago there was a flourishing business in rug patterns and in burlap already prepared with a design.

Today many commercial rug designs are quite handsome but the satisfaction of developing a completely original rug can never be matched. Just think how much your husband would enjoy a rug that incorporated all his hobbies and interests in its design.

MATERIALS

Backing: The traditional material is burlap with a firm, even weave. Other backings are heavy, 2-thread cotton of even weave, similar to monk's cloth, or warp cloth. Whatever the foundation, buy enough to allow at least 2″ extra on all sides of rug for hems. If you have to piece your fabric for a very large rug, overlap edges 2″ and stitch with strong thread before beginning to hook. Then simply hook through the overlapping thicknesses.

Filling Material: Wool, cotton, jute, rayon and other synthetic fabrics and rug yarns can be used. The traditional filling is woolen fabric, old or new, cut in strips, but cotton, silk, felt, jersey or other materials with good color and wearing quality can be used. For even wear, it is recommended that you do not use a variety of materials in one rug.

Use any fabrics that are suitable in color or can be dyed for your particular rug. They may be unworn parts of discarded garments or new materials such as mill ends. If wool materials are to be stored for any length of time, protect them against moths.

Cut fabric strips on straight of grain. Avoid seams when cutting garments and do not join strips. Cut material into strips about ⅛″ to ⅜″ wide. The wider strips are used for informal, quickly made rugs, while very narrow strips are used for intricate, delicate patterns. There are cloth cutting machines that cut several strips evenly at a time; also pre-cut strips are available in some shops or from mail-order suppliers. Cut strips 6″ or less in length to blend colors for a neutral effect. When using the same color for quite a distance, the length of the strip does not matter.

Although the amount of material varies somewhat with the individual worker, and greatly with the height of loops, a rough estimate of about half a pound of cut wool strips or heavy wool rug yarn to one square foot of rug is average with ¼″-high loops.

EQUIPMENT

Hooks: There are two main types of rug hooks. One, called a hand hook, resembles a crochet hook set in a wooden handle. Hand hooks vary in length and size of handles, so choose one that fits your hand comfortably and is easy to work with. When using a hand hook, work from the front of the rug. This hook allows greater versatility in design, length of loops, and choice of materials. It is a relaxing way to work, but is slower than using an automatic hook.

There are two kinds of automatic hooks, which are sold with manufacturers' directions. One is a punch needle which can be adjusted to make different length loops and hooks yarn only. The other is a shuttle hook which works with yarn or fabric strips and is operated with two hands in an alternating motion. When using either of the automatic hooks, work from the back of the rug.

Frames: Some people who use a hand hook work without a frame. When automatic hooks are used, a frame must be used because the backing must be taut.

Use a purchased frame that tilts at any desired angle and stands at an easy working height. Some have adjustable roller bars at top and bottom that make it easy to turn the backing to work one part of the design at a time and to roll up the finished work as it is completed.

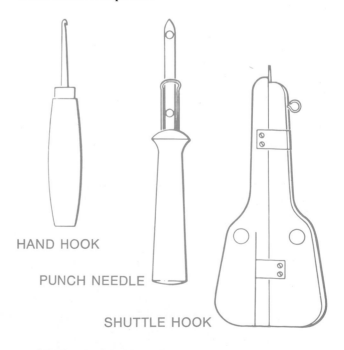

HAND HOOK

PUNCH NEEDLE

SHUTTLE HOOK

Hooked rugs can be adapted to your needs. The ambitious needlewoman can convert this to a round rug, or it can be finished with a border across the top to become an inviting hearth rug.

If you do not want to invest in a frame, you can make one yourself. This may be simply four strips of wood clamped together at the corners with C-clamps. Or make one from strips of 1"×2" lumber. Cut side pieces about 4 feet long and cross pieces about 2 feet long. Drill ½" holes 3" apart down center of each strip. Lay pieces to form size of frame desired and fasten with wooden pegs or bolts through holes where strips cross. To use frame, place it across the backs of chairs so it will be at a comfortable working height when you are seated. To mount canvas on this frame, you can lace through the holes with heavy cord, or the backing can simply be thumbtacked to the crossbars. (Purchased frames come with instructions for mounting backing.)

METHOD

Transferring the Design: If you want to use your own design rather than a purchased backing upon which the design has already been drawn, use a wax crayon or felt-tipped pen to draw the lines on the backing. If you are using a hand hook, draw the design on the right side of the rug; if using an automatic hook, draw it on the wrong side.

Mark off the outside measurements of the rug, being sure to allow all around for hems. Follow the lengthwise and crosswise threads of the fabric. For a straight-edge rug, use a ruler to make sure you get straight edges. Make an actual-size drawing of the design on wrapping paper and transfer it to the backing with carbon paper. Then go over the impression with crayon or pen. You can also indicate colors to be used on the backing. Lines will be hidden in the work when the rug is hooked.

Hooking: If using a hand hook, hold the yarn or strip of fabric between the thumb and index finger of left hand under the backing. Grasp hook in palm of right hand. With palm down, insert hook from top through a mesh of the backing, meeting the strip held in back. Draw end of strip through (always have the ends on top). Skip a few threads of backing; insert hook and draw up a loop to the height

desired. Remove hook from loop and with left hand adjust the loop. Continue drawing up loops until you reach the end of the strip. Draw end to right side; clip end even with loops. (Most people work a large area before they clip the ends.) Have loops close enough to cover the backing, but not so close that rug will cup or buckle. Hook outline of design first, then fill it in. Work the background last.

Special Effects: Clipped rugs are made by cutting each loop individually. Although these rugs do not wear as well as unclipped rugs, many people prefer them for their velvety pile.

Sculptured rugs can be made by shearing the tops of some loops lower than others. Shearing must be done with great care.

Textured effects can be obtained by drawing loops to different heights.

FINISHING

If rug is to be made without a frame, you can turn under hems before starting to hook. To do this, turn under hems all around, following line drawn for edge of rug. Sew hem flat with several rows of basting. Then hook through both thicknesses out to the edge. On rugs made on a frame, simply turn hems under when hooking is completed and sew in place. Sew or iron on rug binding over hem, if desired.

A special liquid may be applied to seal hooking and prevent rug from slipping on the floor. Sold in most needlework departments, it is brushed or sprayed on the back of the rug. If you prefer, you may line your rug with burlap or heavy muslin.

CARE OF HOOKED RUGS

Most hooked rugs can be treated just like other good rugs. They can even be vacuumed. Cleaners usually shampoo all but shaggy rugs, which should be naphtha cleaned. Cotton rugs on a cotton backing can be washed in a machine, but if made on burlap they should be dry cleaned, as burlap shrinks.

You can shampoo a hooked rug at home by using one of the rug shampooers on the market which work something like a carpet sweeper, spraying shampoo onto the rug as it is moved back and forth. Be sure to follow the directions which come with the shampooer.

ROUND HOOKED RUG

Here's a colorful hooked rug design that can grow as large as your needlework ambitions. To begin with, try it in its present little size as a welcome mat or even as a half-circle hearth rug. As your skill

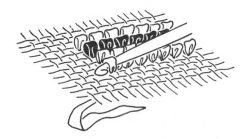

—and speed—develop, make another rug, adding outer circles of the large and small flowers to create a handsome floor covering for a dining area or to enhance a conversation grouping in your living room.

SIZE: 36″ in diameter.

MATERIALS: 1¼ yards 39″-40″ rug burlap; 1 oz. skeins wool rug yarn, 16 garnet, 12 grape, 12 pink; 1¼ yards 39″ to 40″ burlap or heavy muslin for lining; heavy thread.

EQUIPMENT: Hand or automatic hook; rug frame (optional with hand hook); rug needle.

DESIGN: Enlarge diagram for design (each small square = 1″ square). One quarter of design is given. Complete design and transfer to burlap, placing de-

sign so that equal margins are left on sides and on ends. Leave selvages and baste temporary hems on ends to prevent fraying.

HOOKING: Place work in frame if one is being used. Hook loops to a height of ⅜″ throughout. All flowers are worked in pink and grape. Border lines are pink. Centers of large flowers are garnet and all background areas are garnet. See photograph for light (pink) and dark (grape) areas. Loops are left unclipped.

FINISHING: Cut out rug, leaving 1½″ to 2″ hem allowance all around. Cut lining same size. Turn under and baste hem allowances on both pieces. Pin lining to back of rug and whip together around edge.

Knitting

No one can say that the art of knitting goes quite as far back as Adam and Eve—but if there hadn't been fig trees in the Garden of Eden, it's possible that mankind would have begun to knit even earlier! As it is, the history of knitting is one of the most fascinating of all the hand arts.

Supposedly Arabic in origin, knitting found its way into many parts of the world long before Columbus set sail on that fateful voyage. Bits of knitting found their way into Egyptian tombs.

Perhaps the most inspiring legend about knitting is that Christ's famous seamless garment worn on His way to Calvary was a knitted one. If it had been woven, the Roman soldiers quite possibly might have cut it up and meted out the precious pieces. Instead, since cutting a knitted garment would have raveled it, they cast lots for it, so the Bible tells us.

No matter what the history and background of knitting may be, it is still second only to basic sewing as a useful needlecraft to know. If you had lived in an earlier era, you would have learned to knit before you learned your ABC's. Unfortunately mothers are often unable to impart this practical skill to their young daughters and grandmothers today may be off waterskiing in Acapulco. So let the following pages take the place of a kindly grandmother and give you the knitting skills that will provide you endless hours of relaxation as well as a source for beautiful sweaters, baby garments, afghans and a supply of wonderful gifts.

Hand knitting is the technique of drawing loops of yarn through loops already on a knitting needle to form a webbing or fabric. This fabric has greater elasticity than a woven one. By manipulating the basic stitches in various yarns and threads one can produce an infinite variety of patterns from cobwebby lace to heavy rugs.

MATERIALS

Although we usually think of wool yarn when we think of knitting, any type of thread or yarn may be used. Fine cotton thread is used for knitting lace, heavier cottons for bedspreads and rugs. Wool in its great variety is used for sweaters, suits, coats, afghans. Now fascinating synthetics are available so that many garments may be machine washable.

In any case, use the yarn specified in the direc-

tions. Only the expert knitter should attempt substitutions. Purchase all the yarn needed for your project at one time. Later dye lots may differ slightly in color and weight and produce perceptible variations in your work.

EQUIPMENT

Knitting needles vary in size from a little thicker than a straight pin to a giant 1″ in diameter. They may be made of aluminum, steel, plastic or wood. The small number indicates a fine needle; the large number indicates a large needle. Directions will always specify the needles to use.

Single-pointed needles come in pairs and are used to knit back and forth in rows. They are readily available in 10″ and 14″ lengths. Other lengths may be found, however. Sizes run 0, 1, 2, 3, 4, 5, 6, 7, 8, 9, 10, 10½, 11, 13, 15, 17, 19, 35 and 50. These are American sizes. If you have an old collection of needles, they may indicate English sizes. Be sure that you determine their size by comparing them with some needles in a knitting shop or department store, or using a purchased needle gauge (a piece of plastic punched with needle holes numbered according to size).

Double-pointed needles come in sets of four and are used to knit in the round such things as socks, mittens and neckbands on sweaters. They come in 7″ and 10″ lengths but may occasionally be found in other lengths. Sizes run from 0 to 8 in aluminum and from 1 to 15 in plastic.

Circular needles are used to knit skirts and other comparatively wide items in the round. They are also used to hold a great number of stitches—more than would fit on a straight needle—and may be used for knitting back and forth. They are readily available in 11″, 16″, 24″, 29″ and 36″ lengths and are occasionally found in very short lengths. The 11 , 16″ and 24″ lengths go up to size 10½; the 29″ and 36″ lengths go up to size 15.

Jumper needles are flexible needles used when a great many stitches are being knitted and are easier to handle than a circular needle.

Many other knitting accessories are available and may be convenient to use. For the beginner simple household items can be substituted, however. Safety pins make good stitch holders. Instead of commercial point guards, rubber bands can be twisted around the points of your needles to prevent the stitches from sliding off when you put away your work. Bobbins can be made of stiff cardboard.

METHOD

How To Cast On

For a practice piece, use knitting worsted and No. 6 needles. Make a slip loop and insert point of needle through it. Tighten loop. Hold needle in left hand. Hold second needle in right hand, with yarn in working position. Insert point of right needle into loop on left needle from left to right, shown above. With index finger bring the yarn over the point of right needle. Draw the yarn through the loop. Insert left needle through new loop and remove right needle. You now have 2 stitches cast on. Make the third and all succeeding stitches the same way. For a stronger edge, insert right needle between stitches just below left needle instead of through loops. Cast on 15 stitches for a practice swatch. You are now ready to begin knitting.

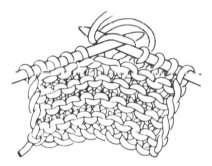

The Knit Stitch

Hold needle with cast-on stitches in your left hand. Insert right needle into front of first stitch on left needle from left to right. With right hand bring yarn under and over the point of right needle and draw the yarn through the stitch; slip the stitch just worked in off the left needle. This completes first stitch of row. Repeat in each stitch.

Always push work along left needle so that stitch to be worked is near tip. When all the stitches have been knitted off left needle, you should have 15 sts on right needle, as you had on the left originally. Count stitches occasionally to make sure that you keep the same number. At the end of row, turn work so needle with stitches is in your left hand. Continue working rows in this manner until you are making the stitches all the same size and you feel familiar with the stitch. When you knit each stitch in each row, it is called **garter stitch**.

To Bind Off

You are now ready to finish off your practice piece. This process is called binding off.

Loosely knit 2 stitches. With point of left needle pick up first stitch and slide it over the second; slip it off needle. * Knit next stitch and slip preceding one over it. Repeat from * across all the stitches.

When you come to your last stitch, cut yarn about 3″ from the needle. Bring loose end through last stitch and pull tightly. Darn in end with tapestry needle so that it will not show.

The Purl Stitch

To make this stitch the yarn is in front of work instead of back, and needle is inserted into stitch from the right instead of left. The wrong side of a purl stitch is a knit stitch. The purl stitch is rarely used alone, so to practice the stitch proceed with stockinette stitch.

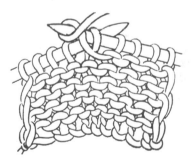

Stockinette Stitch

Cast on 15 stitches for a practice swatch. Knit first row. Turn work. Insert right needle into front of first stitch on left needle from right to left. With right hand bring yarn over the point of right needle and draw yarn through the stitch; slip the stitch just worked into off left needle. This completes the first purl stitch. Keeping yarn in front of work, repeat in each stitch across.

Knit next row, purl next row. Repeat these 2 rows until you are making the stitches all the same size and you feel familiar with the purl stitch. Bind off. (If you bind off on a purl row, purl the stitches instead of knitting them.)

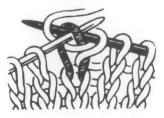

How to Increase

Increases are usually used to shape garments. First work knit (or purl) stitch as usual into front of stitch but leave stitch on left needle. Then knit (or purl) into back of this same stitch.

How to Decrease

There are two ways of decreasing and directions will tell you which one to use.

The first, and most often used way, is when the directions say "dec 1" and specify where to do it. To dec 1, simply knit (or purl) two stitches together as one stitch. This is also what is meant when directions say "k 2 tog (or p 2 tog)".

The second way is when the directions say "sl 1, k 1, psso". (Slip 1, knit 1, pass slipped stitch over.) To do this, slip 1 stitch (simply pass the stitch from left needle to right needle without working it), knit the next stitch, then pass the slipped stitch over the knit stitch.

To Make A Yarn Over

Yarn over automatically increases a stitch and is used mostly in lace patterns, since it produces a hole in the work.

On a knit row, bring yarn under tip of right needle, up and over needle, then work the next stitch.

On a purl row, bring yarn over right needle, around and to front again, then work the next stitch.

A yarn over forms an extra loop on right needle. On the next row, work it as a regular stitch.

How To Attach A New Yarn

Plan to attach new yarn at beginning of a row. Tie a single knot around old yarn, then knit several stitches with new yarn. Pull up old yarn so first stitch is same length as other stitches and knot again. When work is completed, weave both ends into the back of knitting.

How to Pick Up Dropped Stitches

Beginners and even advanced knitters often drop a stitch or stitches. They must be picked up or they will "run" just like a stocking.

Use a crochet hook. Catch the loose stitch and draw the horizontal thread of the row above through it. When picking up a knit stitch, insert hook through first stitch from front to back.

To pick up a purl stitch, insert hook through first stitch from back to front.

Repeat until you reach the row on which you are working, then place stitch on needle.

How to Pick Up Stitches Along an Edge.

With right side of work facing you, tie yarn to spot where picking up is to start. Work with yarn and only one needle. Insert point of needle through knitting a short distance from the edge, wrap yarn around needle as if to knit and draw loop through. Continue in this manner across edge, spacing stitches evenly.

Weaving or Kitchener Stitch

This is a method of joining two pieces of knitting together, such as the tip of a mitten or the toe of a sock. The effect is one of a continuous piece of knitting.

Divide the stitches equally between two needles. Break off yarn leaving about a 15″ end (depending, of course, on the number of stitches to be woven). Thread end into a tapestry needle and work as follows: Hold the 2 needles even and parallel, having the yarn come from the right end of the back needle. Draw tapestry needle through first stitch of front needle as if to purl.

Draw yarn through leaving stitch on needle; draw tapestry needle through first stitch of back needle as if to purl leaving stitch on needle; * draw tapestry needle through first stitch of front needle as if to knit and slip stitch off needle; draw tapestry needle through next stitch on front needle as if to purl but leave stitch on needle; draw tapestry needle through first stitch of back needle as if to purl and slip stitch off needle; draw tapestry needle through next stitch on back needle as if to knit but leave stitch on needle. Repeat from * until all stitches are worked off. Draw end through one remaining stitch and fasten.

You may wish to tighten the woven stitches for a neater finish. Be sure to start with the first woven stitch and work across to the last.

Gauge

It is most important that you knit to the gauge specified in the directions so that your finished article will be the correct size. Gauge means the number of stitches to 1", and may also include the number of rows to 1".

Make a practice piece at least 4" square, using the needles and yarn specified in the direction. With a ruler measure the number of stitches you have to 1". If your stitches do not correspond to the gauge given, experiment with needles of different size.

Abbreviations

beg	beginning
dec	decrease
dp	double pointed
inc	increase
k	knit
p	purl
pat	pattern
psso	pass slipped stitch over
rnd	round
sk	skip
sl	slip
st	stitch
sts	stitches
tog	together
yo	yarn over

Knitting Terminology

Multiple of stitches: A pattern often requires an exact number of stitches, to be worked properly. When the directions say, for example, "multiple of 6 sts," it means the number of stitches must be divisible by 6 — 12, 18, 24, etc. "Multiple of 6 sts plus 3" would be 15, 21, 27, etc.

Place a marker in work: This phrase means to mark with a safety pin a certain point in the work itself to use as a guide in taking future measurements.

Place a marker on needle: This means to place a safety pin, paper clip or purchased plastic stitch marker on the needle between the stitches at the point specified. It is slipped from one needle to the other on subsequent rows.

Slip a stitch: Sometimes also "sl 1", this means that you are to insert the right needle in stitch to be slipped as if to purl and pass it from left to right needle without working it.

Work even: This means to continue working without increasing or decreasing, always keeping the pattern as it has been established.

Repeat from *: This means that all instructions following the * are to be repeated as many times as specified in the directions.

Parentheses ( ): This is used in two ways: To enclose directions for larger sizes as listed at the start of each set of directions, and to indicate that the instructions which they enclose are to be repeated the number of times stated immediately after. For example, (k 2, p 1) twice means that you should knit 2, purl 1, knit 2, and purl 1.

How To Read Charts

Charts are sometimes given to clarify directions as given or as a substitute for what would be very involved directions. They are generally used when a design is to be worked with more than one color, less frequently when the design is worked in one color but with a change of stitch. In either case, simply think of each little square on the chart as one stitch in your work. Usually, the first row of the chart is read from right to left, the second from left to right, and so on.

Working Designs In Color

There are two methods of achieving color patterns on a background. One, sometimes referred to as "Fair Isle knitting," involves using two or more colors of yarn and changing colors every few stitches while knitting. The other is to work a design on top of a piece of knitting in Duplicate Stitch.

When knitting with more than one color of yarn, always carry the yarn not in use at the back of the work. If the unused strand is to be carried more than 3 stitches, twist it with the yarn in use every 3 stitches to avoid having long loops at the back. When changing colors, pick up the strand to be used from under the dropped strand. Be careful not to draw yarn too tightly, or work will pucker.

To work a design on top of a knit piece, thread a tapestry needle with the desired contrasting color. Draw yarn from wrong to right side through center of lower point of stitch. Insert needle at top right-hand side of same stitch. Then, holding needle in horizontal position, draw through to top left side of stitch. Insert again into base of same stitch. Keep yarn loose enough so it completely covers the knit stitch being worked over.

How to Block

To ensure a smooth, professional look, block the knit pieces before sewing them together. Blocking is the process of steaming and shaping a garment. Two similar pieces (sleeves, for example) may be blocked together at the same time. With wrong side up (or right sides together, if working with two pieces), pin to padded board with rustproof pins or thumbtacks placed at ¼" to ½" intervals. Pin to desired measurements. Place a damp cloth over knit piece and press with hot iron, raising it as you move it rather than sliding it back and forth. Don't press down too hard, especially on patterned pieces. Allow to dry thoroughly before unpinning.

BABY SACQUES

There's nothing like getting a good start in the world! What better way to instill a sense of fashion than to begin the high chair crowd with smartly tailored sacques. For the unisex look we have made "his" and "her" sacques—one trimmed with bright pink, one with bright blue.

The beginning knitter will find this an ideal early project. The sacque is made in just one piece and is in simple stockinette stitch throughout. The trim is just bias tape and the easiest of embroidery stitches applied to the finished little garment.

SIZE: Infants' 6 months.
MATERIALS: For each sacque: Nylon or other synthetic baby yarn; 1 package double-fold bias tape; small amount embroidery thread.
EQUIPMENT: Knitting needles, 1 pair No. 3; crewel needle.
GAUGE: 8 sts = 1″; 11 rows = 1″.
BACK: Cast on 88 sts. Work in stockinette st (k on right side, p on wrong side) until piece measures 7″ to underarm, ending on wrong side.

To Shape Sleeves: Cast on 42 sts at beg of next row, k across—130 sts. Cast on 42 sts at beg of next row, p across—172 sts. Work even until sleeves measure 4″ above cast-on rows, ending on wrong side.

To Shape Neck: K across 73 sts, join another strand of yarn, bind off center 26 sts for back of neck, work across remaining sts. Place marker at end of each sleeve for shoulder line.

FRONTS: Working both sides, work even for 1″. Inc 1 st at each neck edge on next row, then every other row twice more. Cast on 2 sts at each neck edge once, then 8 sts once—86 sts on each front. Work even until fronts measure 4″ from shoulder markers, ending at sleeve edge.

To Shape Sleeves: Bind off 42 sts at beg of next 2 rows—44 sts on each front. Work even until fronts measure same as back. Bind off.

FINISHING: Block piece. Sew side and sleeve seams. Bind edges of sacque with bias tape as follows: Starting at left neck edge, stitch tape down front, across lower edge and up right front. Leaving a 9″ length of tape on each front edge for ties, bind neck edge. Bind sleeve edges. (**Note:** When sewing tape in place, be careful not to stretch or pucker knitting.)

With embroidery thread in a color to match or contrast with bias tape, work a line of decorative stitches on all tape (except ties). Holbein stitch was used on pink tape, (shown above in the photograph), chain stitch on blue tape (shown below in the photograph).

STRIPED AFGHAN

This brightly striped afghan is easy to make yet gives the inexperienced knitter excellent practice in changing colors frequently. There is no complicated pattern to remember, however, and you will soon be able to work on your afghan and still watch television out of the corner of your eye.

SIZE: About 40"×54" not including fringe.

MATERIALS: Knitting worsted, 20 ozs. each of bright blue (A) and bright green (B).

EQUIPMENT: Circular knitting needle No. 10 (29" length); steel crochet hook Size 1/0.

GAUGE: 12 sts = 2"; 11 rows = 2".

NOTE: When changing colors, always twist one around the other.

Beg at narrow end with A, cast on 244 sts. Attach B. **Row 1:** Sl 1 as if to p, with B, k 2, * with yarn in back of work sl 2 as if to p, k 2, repeat from * across, ending k 3. **Row 2:** Sl 1 as if to p, with B, k 2, * with yarn in front of work sl 2 as if to p, k 2, repeat from * across, ending sl 1 as if to p. **Row 3:** With A, k 1, with yarn in back of work sl 2 as if to p, * k 2, with yarn in back of work sl 2 as if to p, repeat from * across, ending k 1. **Row 4:** With A and yarn in front of work, sl 3 as if to p, * p 2, with yarn in front of work sl 2 as if to p, repeat from * across, ending p 1 with B instead of A. Repeat these 4 rows for pat until piece measures 54", ending with Row 2. With B, bind off in p.

FRINGE: Cut two 12" strands A. Double the strands to form a loop. Right side facing, insert crochet hook from back to front through bound-off edge of an A stripe and draw loop through. Draw loose ends through loop and pull up tightly. Matching fringe color to stripe color, tie 2 strands in same way on every stripe across. Trim evenly. Repeat fringe at other end.

KNITTED MITTENS

Here's a cozy pair of mittens for you to knit by two completely different methods. Make a pair each way and you will learn all of the following useful knitting techniques: You will learn to knit with four needles as well as your usual two needle way. You will learn to knit with two colors of yarn and also to apply a design with duplicate stitch. And you will learn Kitchener stitch — a neat way to weave together stitches. Do all this well and you deserve your Ph.D. in knitting!

SIZES: 7¼" around palm.
MATERIALS: Sport yarn, 3 ozs. main color (MC), small amount white.
EQUIPMENT: Knitting needles, 1 pair No. 5 for 2-needle mittens or 1 set No. 5 dp needles for 4-needle mittens; tapestry needle.

2-NEEDLE MITTENS
(Design Knit In)

RIGHT MITTEN: Starting at cuff, with MC, cast on 45 sts. **Row 1** (wrong side): P 2, * k 1, p 2, repeat from * across. **Row 2**: K 2, * p 1, k 2, repeat from * across. Repeat these 2 rows for 2", ending on wrong side and decreasing 1 st at end of last row — 44 sts. Work in stockinette st (k on right side, p on wrong side) for 6 rows.

To Establish Pattern: K 32 sts, attach white and k 2 white, with MC k across. Following chart (each symbol on chart represents 1 st worked in white), continue to work design until it is completed. **At the same time**, when piece measures 4" from beg, end wrong side. Place marker at each end of row for guide.

To Shape Thumb: K 8, place remaining 36 sts on a holder. **Next Row** (wrong side): Cast on 8 sts at beg of row, p across — 16 sts. Work even until thumb measures 2½" above marker, ending on wrong side. **Next Row:** * K 2 tog, repeat from * across. Cut off yarn, leaving an 8" length. Thread needle with this length, draw through remaining sts, pull up tightly, and fasten securely.

To Make Hand: Row 1: With MC, pick up and k 8 sts across cast-on sts of thumb, then k across sts on holder — 44 sts. Keeping design stitches as on chart, continue in stockinette st for 25 more rows (about 3" above marker), ending on wrong side.

To Shape Tip: Place marker between 22nd and 23rd sts and carry marker up every row. **Dec Row 1:** K 1, k 2 tog through back of sts, k to 2 sts before marker, k 2 tog through front of sts, k 2 tog through back of sts, k to within last 3 sts, k 2 tog through front of sts, k 1 — 4 sts decreased. **Next Row:** P across. Repeat these 2 rows until 20 sts remain, ending with a k row. Cut off yarn, leaving a 15" length. Divide sts evenly on 2 needles and weave tog with Kitchener stitch (see general directions).

LEFT MITTEN: Work same as right mitten until 6 rows of stockinette st have been completed.

To Establish Pattern: K 10, attach white and k 2, with MC work across. Working pattern as before, work even until piece measures 4" from beg, ending on right side. Place marker at each end of row for guide.

To Shape Thumb: P 8, place remaining sts on holder. **Next Row** (right side): Cast on 8 sts at beg of row, k across — 16 sts. Complete thumb as for right mitten.

To Make Hand: Row 1 (right side): Keeping design stitches as on chart, with MC, k across sts on holder, pick up and k 8 sts across cast-on sts of thumb — 44 sts. Complete to correspond to right mitten.

FINISHING: Sew tog sides of mittens and of thumb. Steam-press lightly.

4-NEEDLE MITTENS
(Design Embroidered)

RIGHT MITTEN: With MC, cast on 45 sts; divide sts evenly on 3 needles; join, being careful not to twist sts. Place marker at beg of each rnd. **Rnd 1:** K 2, p 1, repeat from * around. Repeat Rnd 1 for 2", decreasing 1 st at end of last rnd — 44 sts. Work in stockinette st (k each rnd) until work measures 4" from beg. Divide sts on 2 needles. Place marker at each end for guide.

To Shape Thumb: K 8 sts, place remaining sts on 2 holders. Cast on 8 sts at end of row — 16 sts. Divide these sts on 3 needles; join. K each rnd until thumb measures 2½" above marker. **Next Rnd:** * K 2 tog, repeat from * around. Cut off yarn, leaving an 8" length. Thread a needle with this length, draw through remaining sts, pull up tightly, and fasten securely.

To Work Hand: With MC, pick up and k 8 sts across cast-on sts of thumb, then k across sts on holders, dividing sts on 3 needles — 44 sts. Place markers directly above first set and carry these up every rnd. Continue in stockinette st for 25 more rnds (about 3" above thumb marker).

To Shape Tip: Dec Rnd 1: K 2 tog through back of sts, k to 2 sts before marker, k 2 tog through front of sts, k 2 tog through back of sts, k to 2 sts before last marker, k 2 tog through front of sts — 4 sts decreased. **Next Rnd:** Knit. Repeat these 2 rnds until 20 sts remain. Cut yarn, leaving a 15" length. Divide sts evenly on 2 needles and weave tog with Kitchener stitch (see general directions).

LEFT MITTEN: Work same as right mitten, reversing the placement of thumb.

FINISHING: Mark center of back of each mitten with a vertical basting thread. Thread needle with white yarn. Starting on the 7th rnd above cuff, embroider design with duplicate stitch (see general directions). Place 1 st on each side of basting line and follow chart from bottom up. Each symbol on chart indicates 1 duplicate stitch.

Crocheting

If it is true that familiarity breeds contempt, we are going to have a tough time convincing you of the intrinsic beauty of crochet. We have all seen too many bad examples of handkerchief edgings and limp doilies to view crochet with a completely unjaundiced eye. Do try to forget the bad examples, however, and you will soon see how lovely a really fine piece of crochet can be.

Crochet (as well as many other forms of needlework) is like the well-known prophet—without honor in his own country. Since crochet was always taken for granted, nothing was done to preserve it or to record its history for later generations. As a result we know little about its origins. We do know, however, that even the most primitive people inevitably manipulate a string to make a series of interlocking loops—a chain. This is the foundation of all crocheting. We can imagine that whenever people, especially children, had a string—perhaps a fiber or a sinew—they would loop it through itself using only the fingers as a tool. As they became more adept at this looping technique they sought for a tool more refined than stubby fingers. Finally the first crochet hook was probably developed from a sliver of bone or wood. From that point on there was no stopping the crocheter.

The big impetus for crocheting came in the first half of the nineteenth century when nuns used their delicate products to obtain a bit of money to feed the starving in famine-stricken Ireland. Their crocheted laces copied from the exquisite needle and bobbin laces of France and Italy had quite a vogue in London and other fashion-minded capitals of Europe. With the great emigration of Irish people to the United States at that time, came the women with samples of their favorite crochet patterns, and the skills to make them. American women were eager to learn the new technique and soon produced miles of crochet that, if laid end to end, would stretch from "sea to shining sea."

Today crochet need not be elaborate to be totally acceptable. A functional pot holder is as significant as a glittery crocheted evening bag. They each serve their purpose. The great variety of uses is one of the most interesting things about crochet. Many of us old-time needleworkers learned to crochet by making the inevitable wash cloth. We learned—and the wash cloth did its job. As we become fascinated by the technique we can produce everything from the filmiest laces to the most luxurious suits. Although there is nothing more to crocheting than pulling one loop through another with a little hook, the variations are endless. Learn the basics and you will find a lifetime of pleasure and fulfillment.

MATERIALS

Although we usually think of cotton when we think of crocheting, the thread or yarn can be of any fiber, natural or man-made. Linen thread would make a cool summer blouse. Wool, of course, is ideal for an afghan, a sweater, a baby carriage cover. The synthetics work up beautifully in any of the preceding items and are often machine washable. But we invariably return to cotton when we do any amount of crocheting. Crochet cottons may be as fine as sewing thread or as thick as cord. It may be mercerized and have a smooth silky finish or it may have the matte appearance of some bedspread cottons.

Always buy all the thread or yarn you need at one time to be sure that you have one dye lot. Even white or ecru threads may vary slightly and the variations will show up in your finished work. Also be sure to check yardages when you are switching from the yarn or thread of one manufacturer to a similar product of another manufacturer. The ball or skein may have an entirely different yardage from the amount you need.

EQUIPMENT

Modern production methods produce crochet hooks of fine quality which are lightweight and comfortable to use. Steel crochet hooks 5″ long are usually used for cotton and come in sizes 00, 0, 1 all the way through 14. Size 00 is the largest, 14 the smallest. Bone hooks are available but are rapidly being supplanted by plastic and aluminum hooks. In fact, aluminum hooks 6″ long are the most readily available today. These are used for slightly heavier types of crocheting (sweaters, pot holders, etc.). They are usually designated by letters and run from B or C through K, K being the largest. The plastic hooks may also be designated by number but these numbers vary from manufacturer to manufacturer.

Afghan hooks are used for a special type of crocheting called afghan stitch. These are plastic or, more commonly today, aluminum. They are 9″ or 14″ long and come in sizes F through J.

Extra large hooks for rugs and jiffy crochet have usually been made of wood and (just to confuse the poor crocheter) are numbered from 10 (the smallest) through 15 (the largest). New jumbo hooks are now available in plastic; Q, for instance, is ⅝″ in diameter.

METHOD

To Begin To Crochet

Make a practice piece of each new stitch and work until you are familiar with it. To practice, use medium-weight thread (a little heavier than bedspread cotton) and a No. 4 steel crochet hook. Make a loop at the end of thread and hold loop in place with thumb and forefinger of left hand. At left is short end of thread; at right is the long or working thread. With right hand, grasp the crochet hook as you would a pencil and put hook through loop, catch working thread and draw it through. Pull short end and working thread in opposite directions to bring loop close around the end of hook. Measure down working thread about 4″ from loop on hook. At this point, insert thread between ring finger and little finger of left hand. Weave thread toward back, under little and ring fingers, over middle finger and under forefinger toward you. Grasp hook and loop with thumb and forefinger of left hand. Gently pull working thread so that it is taut but not tight. Hold hook as you would a pencil, but bring middle finger forward to rest near tip of hook. In order to begin working, adjust fingers of left hand as in Diagram 1. The middle finger is bent so it can control the tension while the ring and little fingers prevent the thread from moving too freely. As you practice, you will become familiar with the correct tension. Now you are ready to begin the chain stitch.

Chain Stitch (ch)

Pass hook under thread and catch thread with hook (Diagram 2). Draw thread through loop on hook. This makes one chain (Diagram 3).

Repeat these two steps until you have as many chain stitches as you need. One loop always remains on hook. Keep thumb and forefinger of your left hand near stitch on which you are working. Practice making chains until they are uniform.

Single Crochet (sc)

Make a foundation chain of 20 stitches for practice piece. Insert hook from front under 2 top threads of 2nd chain from hook (Diagram 4). Pass hook under thread and catch thread with hook to make "thread over". Draw through stitch. Thread over and draw through two loops on hook. One loop remains on hook. One single crochet is now completed. For next single crochet, insert hook under 2 top threads of next stitch (Diagram 5) and continue to work in this manner in each stitch across. At the end of row of single crochet, chain 1 for "turning chain". Turn work so reverse side is facing you. Insert hook under 2 top threads of first single crochet and work across as before. Continue working single crochet in this manner. On the last row do not make a turning chain. Clip thread about 3″ from work, bring loose end through the loop remaining on hook and pull tight.

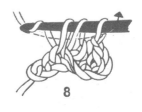

Double Crochet (dc)

Make a foundation chain of 20 stitches for practice piece. Thread over, insert hook under the 2 top threads of 4th chain from hook (Diagram 6). Thread over, draw through stitch. Thread over and draw through 2 loops. Thread over again and draw through 2 remaining loops. One loop remains on hook. One double crochet is now completed (Diagram 7). For next double crochet, thread over, insert hook under the 2 top threads of next stitch and continue to work in this manner in each stitch. At end of row, chain 3 and turn work. On next row, thread over, skip first double crochet, insert hook under the 2 top threads of 2nd double crochet and work across as before. Continue working double crochet in this manner. On the last row do not make a turning chain. Clip thread about 3″ from work, bring loose end through the loop remaining on hook and pull tight.

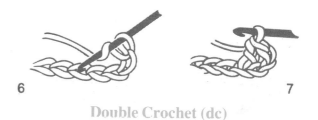

Half Double Crochet (hdc)

To make half double crochet, thread over, insert hook under the 2 top threads of 3rd chain from hook. Three loops are on hook. Thread over and draw through all 3 loops at once (Diagram 8). Half double crochet is now completed. At end of rows, chain 2 to turn.

Treble Crochet (tr)

Make foundation chain of 20 stitches for practice piece. Thread over twice, insert hook under 2 top threads of 5th chain from hook. Thread over and draw a loop through the chain. There are now 4 loops on hook. Thread over again (Diagram 9). Draw through 2 loops on hook. Thread over again and draw through 2 loops. Thread over again (Diagram 10) and draw through 2 remaining loops. One loop remains on hook. One treble crochet is now completed. At end of row, chain 4 to turn. Continue making treble in this manner until you are familiar with the stitch. Finish piece same as for single or double crochet.

Double Treble (d tr)

Thread over hook 3 times, insert hook under 2 top threads of 6th chain from hook and draw a loop through the chain. Five loops are on hook. Thread over and draw through 2 loops four times (Diagram 11). A double treble is now completed. At end of row, chain 5 to turn.

Triple Treble (tr tr)

Thread over hook 4 times, insert hook under 2 top threads of 7th chain from hook and draw a loop

through the chain. Six loops are on hook. Thread over and draw through 2 loops 5 times (Diagram 12). A triple treble is now completed. At end of row, chain 6 to turn.

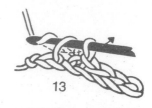

Slip Stitch (sl st)

Make a foundation chain of 20 stitches for practice piece. Insert hook under top thread of 2nd chain from hook, thread over. With one motion, draw through stitch and through loop on hook. Insert hook under top thread of next chain, then thread over and draw through stitch and loop on hook (Diagram 13). Repeat until you have made a slip stitch in each chain. When directions say "join," always use a slip stitch. Insert hook through the 2 top threads of stitch, thread over and draw through stitch and loop on hook.

To Decrease Single Crochet

Work one single crochet to point where 2 loops are on hook. Draw up a loop in next stitch. Thread over, draw through 3 loops at one time.

To Decrease Double Crochet

Work one double crochet to point where 2 loops are on hook. Begin another double crochet in next stitch and work until 4 loops are on hook. Thread over, draw through 2 loops. Thread over, draw through 3 loops.

To Increase

When directions call for an increase, work 2 stitches in one stitch to form the extra stitch.

Working Around The Post

The "post" or "bar" is the vertical or upright section of a stitch. When directions say to make a stitch around the post or bar of a stitch in a previous row, insert the hook around the stitch instead of in top of stitch.

ADDITIONAL CROCHET INFORMATION

Gauge

It is most important that you crochet to the gauge specified so that your finished article will be the correct size. Gauge means the number of stitches to 1″ and the number of rows to 1″.

Make a practice piece at least 2″ square, using the hook and materials specified in the directions. With a ruler, measure the number of stitches you have to 1″. If your stitches do not correspond to the gauge, experiment with a hook of a different size.

Crochet Terminology

Multiple of stitches: A pattern often requires an exact number of stitches, to be worked properly. When the directions say, for example, "multiple of 6 sts," it means the number of stitches must be divisible by 6 — 12, 18, 24, etc. "Multiple of 6 sts plus 3" would be 15, 21, 27, etc.

Work even: This means to continue working without increasing or decreasing.

Repeat from *: This means that all instructions following the * are to be repeated as many times as specified in the directions.

Parentheses ( ): This is used in two ways: To enclose directions for larger sizes as listed at the start of each set of directions, and to indicate that the instructions which they enclose are to be repeated the number of times stated immediately after. For example, (tr, ch 1) twice means that you should make a treble, chain 1, treble, ch 1.

Abbreviations

beg	begin
bl	block
ch	chain
dec	decrease
dc	double crochet
d tr	double treble
h dc	half double crochet
inc	increase
lp	loop
pat	pattern
rnd	round
sc	single crochet
sk	skip
sl	slip
st	stitch
sts	stitches
tog	together
tr	treble
tr tr	triple treble
yo	yarn over

Fastening Ends

After you have completed an article, thread each loose end into a needle and darn it through a solid part of the crochet to fasten it securely. Cut off remaining thread close to the work. Be sure starting ends are long enough to be fastened off.

Blocking

Place article wrong side up on a flat, padded surface. Gently stretch and shape it to the desired measurements. Pin to surface, using rust-proof pins. Place a damp cloth over piece and press with a hot iron, raising it as you move it rather than sliding it back and forth, being careful not to let weight of iron rest on article. Let dry thoroughly before unpinning.

Sewing Edges Together

Pin together edges to be sewed, matching any pattern in rows or stitches. Thread needle with matching thread or yarn. To begin sewing, do not knot thread but take several over and over stitches, darning them, if possible, through a solid part of the crochet. Sew straight even edges with a whipped stitch, placing it at edges of the work. Sew slanting or uneven edges (caused by increasing or decreasing) with a backstitch, placing it just inside edges of work. Leave stitches loose enough to match the elasticity of the crochet. Steam-press seams lightly.

CROCHETED POT HOLDERS

A pot holder may not seem to be a truly inspired crochet project but—if you are a beginner—don't let your ambitions run away with you. If your stitches are not too even, here's a good way to perfect your skill. Leave the crocheted spread for a king-size bed for later.

SIZES: Square pot holders: about 7½" square; round pot holder: about 7½" in diameter.
MATERIALS: For 3 pot holders: Heavy cotton or rayon-and-cotton rug yarn, 70-yard skeins, 1 dark color (DC), and 1 light color (LC).
EQUIPMENT: Aluminum crochet hook size I for square pot holders, H for round pot holders.

SQUARE POTHOLDER IN SINGLE CROCHET

GAUGE: 5 sc = 2".

With size I hook and LC, ch 16. **Row 1:** Sc in 2nd ch from hook, and in each ch across—15 sc. Ch 1, turn. Repeat Row 2 until work measures 6" from beg. Cut off yarn.

Edging: Rnd 1: Join DC in any corner st. Work sc all around, working 1 sc in each st and in each row, and 3 sc in each corner. Join with sl st in first sc. Cut off yarn. Turn. **Rnd 2:** Join LC in any corner st. * Ch 1, sc in next sc, repeat from * around, working sc, ch 1, sc in each corner st. Join with sl st in first st. Cut off yarn. Turn. **Rnd 3:** Join DC in ch-1 sp at any corner. Sc in each ch-1 sp around, working 2 sc in each corner sp. Join with sl st in first sc. Do not turn. Ch 14 tightly, sl st in same sc where joining was made. Cut off yarn. Weave in ends. Steam-press.

ROUND POTHOLDER

GAUGE: 3 sc — 1".

With size H hook and DC, ch 2. **Rnd 1:** Work 8 sc in 2nd ch from hook. Join with sl st in first sc. Ch 1, turn. **Rnd 2:** Sc in first sc, ch 1, * sc in next sc, ch 1, repeat from * around. Join with sl st in first sc—8 ch-1 sps. Cut off yarn. Turn. **Rnd 3:** Join LC in any sc, sc in same sc, ch 1, sc in next ch-1 sp, ch 1, * sc in next sc, ch 1, sc in next ch-1 sp, ch 1, repeat from * around. Join with sl st in first sc. Ch 1. Turn. **Rnd 4:** Sl st in next ch-1 sp, ch 1, sc in same sp, ch 1, * sk next sc, sc in next ch-1 sp, ch 1, repeat from * around. Join with sl st in first sc. Cut off yarn. Turn. **Rnd 5:** Join DC in any ch-1 sp. Work sc, ch 1 and sc in same sp, ch 1, * sk next sc, sc, ch 1 and sc in next ch-1 sp, ch 1, repeat from * around. Join with sl st in first sc—32 sc. Cut off yarn. Turn. **Rnd 6:** Join LC in any ch-1 sp, sc in same sp, ch 1, * sc in next ch-1 sp, ch 1, repeat from * around. Join with sl st in first sc. Ch 1, turn. **Rnd 7:** Sl st in next ch-1 sp, ch 1, sc in same sp, ch 1, * sc in next ch-1 sp, ch 1, repeat from * around. Join in first sc. Cut off yarn, turn. **Rnd 8:** Join DC in any ch-1 sp and work same as Rnd 6. **Rnd 9:** Repeat Rnd 7. Cut off yarn. Turn. **Rnd 10:** Join LC in any sc, sc in same sc, sc in next ch-1 sp, * sc in next sc, sc in next ch-1 sp, repeat from * around. Join with sl st in first sc. Ch 1, turn. **Rnd 11:** Sc in each sc around. Join with sl st in first sc. Do not turn. Ch 14 tightly, sl st in same sc where joining was made. Cut off yarn. Weave in ends. Steam-press.

SQUARE POTHOLDER IN DOUBLE CROCHET

GAUGE: 5 dc = 2".

With size I hook and DC, ch 19. **Row 1:** Dc in 4th ch from hook and in each ch across—17 dc, counting turning ch as 1 dc. Ch 3, turn. **Row 2:** Sk first dc, dc in each dc across, ending with last dc in top of turning ch—17 dc. Ch 3, turn. Repeat Row 2 until work measures 6" from beg. Do not work ch 3 at end of last row. Cut off yarn.

Edging: Join LC in any corner st. Work sc all around, keeping work flat and working 2 sc in each corner. Join with sl st in first sc. Do not turn. Ch 14 tightly, sl st in same sc where joining was made. Cut off yarn. Weave in ends. Steam-press.

LONG MUFFLER

If you have a romantic turn of mind, you might visualize yourself all pink cheeked and swathed in this cozy muffler swooping down a ski slope on a far-away Alp. More likely you'll be glad you have it some blustery morning when you have to drive the kids to school. Either way, this easy-to-make muffler, worked in the rich colors of old stained glass, is a useful adjunct to a winter wardrobe. It will also give you good experience in crochet just one step beyond the basic techniques. In fact, if you want to tackle a slightly more ambitious project, just triple its width and you'll have a handsome afghan!

SIZE: About 15″ × 68″ without fringe.

MATERIALS: Knitting worsted, 6 oz. dark turquoise (A), 10 oz. olive (B), 4 oz. light turquoise (C), and 4 oz. bright blue (D).

EQUIPMENT: Aluminum crochet hook size G.

GAUGE: 4 dc = 1″; 8 rows = 3½″.

NOTE: When changing colors, always work off last 2 lps of last dc with new color, then cut off old color.

With color A, ch 64. **Row 1** (mesh row): Dc in 6th ch from hook for first mesh; * ch 1, sk 1 ch, dc in next ch, repeat from * across—30 meshes. Ch 4, turn. **Row 2** (mesh row): Sk first dc, dc in first mesh, * ch 1, dc in next mesh, repeat from * across, ending last dc in last mesh—30 meshes. Ch 4, turn. **Row 3** (mesh row): Repeat Row 2. Working last 2 lps with color B, ch 3, turn. **Row 4:** Sk first dc, dc in first mesh, * dc in next dc, dc in next mesh, repeat from * across, end dc in last mesh, dc in 3rd ch of turning ch—60 dc. Ch 3, turn. **Row 5:** Sk first dc, work dc in each dc across, ending last dc in top of turning ch. Working last 2 lps with color C, ch 3, turn. **Row 6:** Skip first dc, work dc in each dc across, ending last dc in top of turning ch. Working last 2 lps with color B, ch 3, turn. **Row 7:** Skip first dc, work dc in each dc across, ending dc in top of turning ch. Ch 3, turn. **Row 8:** Repeat Row 7, but working last 3 lps with color A, ch 4, turn. **Row 9** (mesh row): Sk first 2 dc, dc in next dc, * ch 1, sk next dc, dc in next dc, repeat from * across, ending last dc in 2nd ch of turning ch. Ch 4, turn. **Rows 10 and 11** (mesh rows): Repeat Rows 2 and 3. Repeat Rows 4 through 11 for pat in following color order: * 2 rows B, 1 row D, 2 rows B, 3 rows (mesh rows) A, 2 rows B, 1 row D, 2 rows B, 3 rows (mesh rows) A, 2 rows B, 1 row C, 2 rows B, 3 rows (mesh rows) A, repeat from * 5 times. Fasten off.

FINISHING: Steam-press muffler lightly. Weave in all ends.

Fringe: Cut 3 strands color C 10″ long. Double the strands to form a loop. Right side of work facing, insert crochet hook from back to front through a mesh on end of scarf and draw loop through. Draw loose ends through loop and pull up tightly. Knot fringe through each mesh across each end.

CROCHETED TABLECLOTH

Thanksgiving dinner down through the years, a sixteenth birthday party, afternoon tea following a baby shower, all the memorable events that bind a family together could be celebrated around this festive tablecloth. The love and care that you put into making something on this scale will be rewarded many times over by the joy of using a family treasure you have created with your own hands.

SIZE: About 60″ × 80″.
MATERIALS: Mercerized crochet cotton, 19 450-yd. balls white or ecru.
EQUIPMENT: Steel crochet hook No. 9.
GAUGE: Each motif = 4″ square.
FIRST MOTIF: Beg at center, ch 8. Join with sl st to form a ring. **Rnd 1:** Ch 3, 2 dc in ring, (ch 7, 3 dc in ring) 3 times; ch 7, sl st in top of ch-3. **Rnd 2:** Ch 3, dc in next 2 dc, (ch 2, 7 dc in next loop, ch 2, dc in next 3 dc) 3 times; ch 2, 7 dc in next loop, ch 2. Join. **Rnd 3:** Ch 3, dc in next 2 dc, * ch 3, (dc in next dc, ch 1) 6 times, dc in next dc; ch 3, dc in next 3 dc. Repeat from * around, ending ch 3. Join in top of first ch-3. **Rnd 4:** Ch 3, dc in next 2 dc, * (ch 3, sc in next ch-1 sp) 6 times; ch 3, dc in each dc of 3-dc group. Repeat from * around, ending ch 3. Join in top of first ch-3. **Rnd 5:** Ch 3, * in next dc make

2 dc, ch 7 and 2 dc, dc in next dc (corner); (ch 3, sc in next ch-3 loop of pineapple) 5 times; ch 3, dc in next dc. Repeat from * around. Join. **Rnd 6:** Ch 3, * dc in next 2 dc, ch 3, 5 dc in next loop, ch 3, dc in next 3 dc; (ch 3, sc in next ch-3 loop) 4 times; ch 3, dc in next dc. Repeat from * around, ending ch 3. Join in top of first ch-3. **Rnd 7:** Ch 3, * dc in next 2 dc, ch 4, (dc in next dc, ch 1) 4 times, dc in next dc; ch 4, dc in next 3 dc, (ch 3, sc in next ch-3 loop) 3 times; ch 3, dc in next dc. Repeat from * around, ending ch 3. Join in top of first ch-3. **Rnd 8:** Ch 3, * dc in next 2 dc, ch 5, dc in next dc, ch 1, dc in next sp, ch 1, dc in next dc, ch 1, tr in next sp, ch 1, tr in next dc, ch 1, tr in next sp, ch 1, dc in next dc, ch 1, dc in next sp, ch 1, dc in next dc; ch 5, dc in next 3 dc, (ch 3, sc in next ch-3 loop) twice; ch 3, dc in next dc. Repeat from * around, ending ch 3. Join in top of first ch-3. **Rnd 9:** Ch 3, * dc in next 2 dc, ch 7, (dc in next dc, ch 1) twice, dc in next dc; ch 3, dc in next tr, ch 1, in next tr make (tr, ch 2) twice and tr; ch 1, dc in next tr, ch 3, (dc in next dc, ch 1) twice, dc in next dc; ch 7, dc in next 3 dc, ch 3, sc in next ch-3 loop, ch 3, dc in next dc. Repeat from * around, ending ch 3. Join in top of first ch-3. **Rnd 10:** Ch 4, holding back on hook the last loop of each tr, make tr in next 2 dc, thread over and draw through all loops on hook (a tr-cluster made); * ch 11, 3-dc cluster over next 3 dc, ch 3, sl st in tip of cluster (picot), ch 7, skip next dc, dc in next tr, ch 2, in next tr make dc, ch 7 and dc; ch 2, dc in next tr, ch 7, skip next dc, dc cluster over next 3 dc, picot, ch 11, 3-tr cluster over next 3 dc, picot, 3-tr cluster over next 3 dc. Repeat from * around. Join and cut thread.

SECOND MOTIF: **Rnds 1 through 9:** Work as for Rnds 1 through 9 of First Motif. **Rnd 10:** Work as for First Motif until first dc of corner is made, ch 3, sl st in corner loop of First Motif, ch 3, dc in same place as last dc on Second Motif. Continue pattern on Second Motif until next cluster is made, ch 1, sl st in picot of First Motif, ch 1, sl st in tip of cluster on Second Motif. Continue in pattern across Second Motif, joining next 2 picots and next corner as before. Complete as for First Motif (no more joinings). Cut thread.

Make 15 rows of 20 motifs, joining adjacent sides as Second Motif was joined to First Motif. Where 4 corners meet, join 3rd and 4th corners to joining of previous 2 corners.

Edging: With right side facing, attach thread to corner lp at joining of any 2 motifs, ch 3, in same lp make 2 dc, ch-5 picot and 3 dc, * sc in next sp, ch 3, in next lp (sc, ch 3) twice, sc in same lp, in next picot make 3 dc, ch-5 picot, 3 dc (shell), sc in next lp, (ch 3, sc) 3 times in same lp, shell in next picot, in next lp make (sc, ch 3) 3 times, sc in same lp, shell in next picot, (sc, ch 3) twice, sc in same lp, ch 3, sc in next lp, shell in next joining. Repeat from * around, making 5-dc picot and 5 dc at each outer corner of cloth. Join and cut thread.

FINISHING: Starch cloth lightly and press.

CROCHETED BEDSPREAD

The chef-d'oeuvre of any crochet expert is a bed-spread, and making this handsome spread with its quality of heavily encrusted lace will label you a veritable master of the art. Actually it is not too difficult to crochet even though it uses a great variety of stitches. The repeats are simple to follow and the pattern is really rather easy to remember. You will also find the spiral fringe fun to crochet.

SIZES: Single-bed size, 70″ × 105″ (including fringe); double-bed size, 90″ × 105″ (including fringe).

MATERIALS: Mercerized knitting and crochet cotton, 250-yard balls white, ecru or cream: 66 for single-bed size, 86 for double-bed size.

EQUIPMENT: Steel crochet hook No. 7; tapestry needle.

GAUGE: Each motif = 5″ square.

MOTIF: Beg at center, ch 6. Join with sl st to form ring. **Rnd 1:** Ch 3, 15 dc in ring. Join with sl st to top of ch-3. **Rnd 2:** Ch 8, dc in same place as sl st, * (ch 1, dc in next dc) 3 times; ch 1, in next dc make dc, ch 5 and dc (corner). Repeat from * around. Join last ch 1 to 3rd ch of ch-8. **Rnd 3:** Sl st in next loop, ch 3, 4 dc in same loop, remove hook, insert it in 3rd ch of ch-3 and draw dropped loop through (pc st made), ch 5, 5 dc in same corner loop, remove hook, insert it in first dc and draw dropped loop through (another pc st); * (ch 1, pc st in next ch-1 sp) 4 times; ch 1, in corner loop make pc st, ch 5 and pc st. Repeat from * around, end ch 1. Join last ch 1 to tip of first pc st. **Rnd 4:** Sl st in next loop, ch 4, in same loop make 2 tr, ch 5 and 3 tr; * 2 dc in tip of next 6 pc sts, in corner loop make 3 tr, ch 5 and 3 tr. Repeat from * around. Join to top of ch-4. **Rnd 5:** Sl st in next tr, ch 4, * in corner loop make (tr, ch 1) twice and tr; ch 5, in same corner loop make (tr, ch 1) 3 times; dc in next tr, (ch 1, skip 1 st, dc in next st) 8 times, ch 1. Repeat from * around. Join last ch 1 to 3rd ch of ch-4. **Rnd 6:** Sl st in next sp, ch 3, pc st in same sp, (ch 1, pc st in next sp) twice; ch 1, * in corner loop make (tr, ch 1) twice and tr; ch 5, in same corner loop make (tr, ch 1) 3 times; (pc st in next sp, ch 1) 14 times. Repeat from * around. Join last ch 1 to tip of first pc st. **Rnd 7:** Sc in same place as sl st, sc in next 2 pc sts, * (pc st in next sp, ch 1) 3 times; in corner loop make 3 dc, ch 2, 2 tr, ch 5, 2 tr, ch 2 and 3 dc; (ch 1, pc st in next sp) 3 times; sc in tip of next 14 pc sts. Repeat from * around. Join. **Rnd 8:** Ch 6, * skip 1 sc, tr in next sc, ch 1, dc in next pc st, ch 1, half dc in next pc st, ch 1, sc in next pc st, sc in next 3 dc of corner, 2 sc in next sp, sc in next 2 tr, in next loop make 3 sc, ch 5 and 3 sc; sc in next 2 tr, 2 sc in next sp, sc in next 3 dc, sc in pc st, ch 1, half dc in next pc st, ch 1, dc in next pc st, ch 1, tr in next sc, (ch 1, skip 1 sc, d tr in next sc) 5 times; ch 1. Repeat from * around. Join to 5th ch of ch-6. Cut thread.

For Single Size Spread, make 12 rows of 20 motifs. **For Double Size Spread,** make 16 rows of 20 motifs.

FINISHING: Sew motifs neatly together. Block to measurements.

Fringe: With right side of bedspread facing and working along long side, attach thread to ch-5 corner loop, * (ch 67, turn; 2 sc in 2nd ch from hook and in each ch across—fringe made—sc in next 5 sts of bedspread) 8 times; sc in each st to next joining. Repeat from * around 3 sides of spread, making corners as before. Cut thread.

Finishing Touches

Needleworkers are almost always blessed with generous spirits. They want to share their ideas, patterns, experiences and pleasures with you. There is space here for only a few suggestions that we hope will be helpful.

HEMMING

On household linens you probably trued up the fabric and basted a hem before doing the needlework. If not, baste in a hem of the desired width, mitering corners as described in the directions immediately following. Thread a sewing needle with sewing thread of a color to match your fabric. Place work wrong side up with hem edge toward you. Work from right to left. Fasten thread in fold of hem. Take a tiny stitch (1 or 2 threads of fabric) in the piece itself, then slide needle along ⅛" to ¼" inside the fold of the hem. Repeat, keeping stitches even. Secure the last stitch by making several stitches one on top of the other; run thread through hem and clip off.

Some experts prefer a more pronounced hem. On coarse linens or cottons they work a stitch in every thread of their background fabric. This emphasizes the line where the hem is stitched.

MITERING HEMS

For neat corners on napkins, tablecloths and such items miter the hems as follows:

1. Crease along inside and outside hem lines (A and B in Diagram 1).
2. Unfold hem and clip off corner diagonally (dotted line, Diagram 1).
3. Turn down corner (Diagram 2).

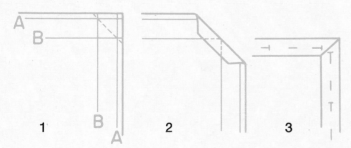

4. Now refold hem along lines A, then lines B. Pin, baste and sew hem, slip-stitching along miter at each corner (Diagram 3).

Helpful Hint: Never use permanent knots at the ends of threads in any form of needlework. To start a new thread leave a 2" end, hold it out of the way on *top* of work until your first few stitches have been made. Later draw end to back of work, insert it in a needle and slip it under a few stitches. Also draw final ends of thread through a few stitches on the back of work and clip off.

WASHING EMBROIDERY

If your needlework has become soiled during the making and it is made of washable and colorfast fabric and threads, it can be hand laundered successfully. Just gently swish the piece through warm water and mild soap suds. Do not squeeze or twist. Rinse thoroughly in clear water. Do not wring out. Roll up loosely in a clean towel. When piece is ready, press or block.

Note: If piece cannot be washed, remove spots and freshen it up with cleaning fluid or take it to a fine dry cleaner.

PRESSING EMBROIDERY

Use a well-padded ironing board and a steam iron or a regular iron and a press cloth. Place embroidery face down and steam press lightly, being careful not to allow the weight of the iron to flatten embroidery. Press the rest of your piece—hems, etc.—as you would any linen or cotton item.

BLOCKING EMBROIDERY

If your needlework has been made in a frame, has been kept clean and does not require hemming or other finishing, it will probably need only blocking to prepare it for framing or the like. Leave it in the embroidery frame (or large hoop), lay a clean wet cloth on the right side of the piece and allow it to remain until dry.

If you have had to wash your embroidery, mark out the exact size of the piece on heavy paper mounted on a large board. While piece is still wet, but not dripping, line up with your marked area. Fasten with rust-proof push pins or thumb tacks at each corner, then in the center of each of the 4 sides. Keep adding pins halfway between those just added, alternating sides, until they are no more than ½″ apart. Allow to dry thoroughly.

Just a Suggestion: If you are left-handed, you may need to adapt a stitch or technique to your own way of doing things. If a stitch diagram is difficult to adapt, try holding a little mirror along the side of the diagram and at a right angle to the page. The mirror image may be easier for you to follow.

FRAMING NEEDLEWORK

We'll assume that you made your embroidery to fit a given frame or that you have found a frame of the proper size and proportions to fit your needlework. Remember that a frame should be large enough to allow a certain amount of plain fabric to extend beyond the embroidered area. This fabric border is usually the same width on top and sides, just a little wider at the bottom. On modern pictures the fabric border may be even all around or omitted entirely.

Remove all little wire nails, hooks and picture wire at back of frame. Refinish frame if necessary.

Cut a piece of firm cardboard to fit into the rabbet which holds the picture at the back of the frame but make it just a hair's breadth narrower all around. Place cardboard in desired position on back of embroidery; draw excess fabric over it. Insert a few straight pins into each edge of cardboard to anchor fabric. If the extra fabric is more than 1½″ to 2″ wide, trim evenly. Make sure that the threads of the background fabric line up squarely on the front of the picture, then fasten down the extra fabric at the top and bottom of the back with masking tape. Repeat at each side of picture.

In some cases if the double folds of fabric at the corners are too bulky, cut away the under layer. This is necessary with certain heavy or stiff fabrics like needlepoint canvas.

Insert the cleaned and polished glass in the frame, then place the picture face down in the frame. Fasten picture in place by carefully hammering a fine wire nail into the center of each side of the rabbet. Larger frames require 2 or 3 nails per side. If a dust cover is desired, run a line of glue around the back of the frame and lay a sheet of brown paper over the entire back. Trim paper close to frame. Replace hooks or picture wire.

A Good Idea: If it is difficult to find suitable background fabric for embroidery, take a look at artists' canvas available by the yard in art supply stores. It is often 54″ wide, comes in both cotton and linen and has a good texture.

MAKING WALL HANGINGS

The easiest way to make a wall hanging is as follows: True up the edges of your needlework piece. Machine stitch or sew by hand narrow hems on the sides, then on the lower edge of your piece. Finally turn down a hem 1″ (or more) wide at the top of the hanging; stitch across, leaving ends of hem open. Width of turn-down depends on thickness of dowel or metal rod that you are using. Insert dowel or rod in top hem. If desired, dressmaker's weights can be sewed to the back of the hanging spaced evenly along the lower edge. Another way to keep the bottom of the wall hanging from buckling is to make the lower hem like the top hem to accommodate a matching dowel or rod. The ends of the dowels can be whittled down to fit into large wooden beads if a decorative trim is desired.

A slightly more complicated way of making a wall hanging is described in the directions for the Butterfly Wall Hanging in the Pretend Appliqué section. The more professional results are well worth the little extra effort. Adapt the directions to any size wall hanging by using the appropriate number of hanging tabs of a size suitable for the piece.

Index